A Broad
ABROAD

Surviving (and Loving)
Your Junior Year
on Foreign Soil

by

Diane Giombetti Clue

BROAD HORIZONS

Broad Horizons
P.O. Box 958
Upton, MA 01568
www.abroadabroadjya.com

The events that take place in this book are true, and the characters in it are all real people. I've changed a few names to protect some folks' privacy.

Memorabilia featured on the cover belongs to Diane Giombetti Clue.
All photos in this book were taken by and belong to Diane Giombetti Clue.

Cover and book design: Holly Mason
Editing: Linda Dini Jenkins

Printed in the United States of America

Library of Congress Control Number: 2015903919

ISBN 978-0692402146

FIRST EDITION

For Colin

Wish you were here.

Twenty years from now you will be
more disappointed by the things you
didn't do than by the ones you did do.
So throw off the bowlines, sail away from
the safe harbor. Catch the trade winds
in your sails. Explore. Dream. Discover.

— Mark Twain

The Board of the University of Kent in America* is delighted to be involved in the publication of this book, and to recommend it as a fantastic resource for any traveler, student, traveling student, and everything else besides.

Many of our members are former JYA and exchange students ourselves and the unique yet universal insights Diane has collected here help us to reminisce fondly about the excitement, the trepidation and, often, the complete bafflement we felt as students in a foreign country. It is at once both a practical guidebook, with invaluable tips told warmly and with humor, as if to a friend, and a personal perspective on the indelible University of Kent experience. In this way this book has been for us both an educational and a nostalgic experience; it reminds us that Kent was, indeed, a life-changing experience that we will never forget!

We hope that you, reader, will find it equally useful and entertaining, and that your own experiences and memories will be re-awoken by it as ours have been.

— *John Hern (Keynes 1980), President of the Board*

*The University of Kent has more than 4,500 alumni currently living and working in America. The University of Kent in America is a separate organization run for and by Kent alumni to help them connect, interact with the University and fundraise for current students where possible. To find out more about the group, or to get involved, visit: www.kent.ac.uk/alumni/UKA

Prologue

When I was a college student back in the mid 1980s, "wired" meant that you'd had way too much caffeine. Blackberries were what you put on your cereal. "Yahoo" was something you yelled when you were excited. And apps were what you ate before your entrée. It was a quieter time, without all of today's hand-held gizmos that beep, blink, ring, and chime.

During my freshman year, only one of the women on my floor had her own word processor. It was a huge, space-hogging monster that crashed every time she created a document longer than 10 pages. The rest of us made do with our IBM Selectric typewriters that our parents had bought for us, or we signed up for time slots to use the college's word processing lab. Most of us still wrote the drafts of our essays and research papers in longhand before typing the final documents.

You were considered high-tech if you had a phone in your dorm room, and some of us didn't. CDs had only just come on the market and were still a novelty. Netflix didn't exist.

Despite all that, we still managed to have an awful lot of low-tech fun. If you're my age (or older), reading this book will probably inspire nostalgia for your own study abroad experience. Younger readers will wonder how we survived without laptops and 24-hour Internet access. Either way, I'm pretty sure you'll laugh.

Enjoy. Diane

Part One

✦ **MICHAELMAS TERM** ✦

✧ Chapter One ✧

I woke up to the voice of the pilot announcing that if we looked out our windows, we'd be able to see England below us. For a moment, I forgot where I was, but the ache in my neck, the stale air, and the roar of the plane's engines quickly reminded me. I had a window seat, so I eagerly raised the shade and looked out.

Below me was a patchwork of brown, green, and yellow squares that looked like a gigantic quilt. Many of the squares were separated from each other by thick hedges. Every once in a while there was a lone tree or a stand of several trees in the middle of one of the squares. As we got closer to Gatwick, the fields gave way to roads, lots of houses, and eventually the airport itself. The wheels hit the tarmac, we bumped down the runway, and I thought to myself, *Holy crap, this is it – there's no turning back now.*

It was October of 1986, and I had just done the bravest thing in my (then) 20 years on this earth: I'd said goodbye to my family and friends, and left absolutely everything I knew behind me to spend my junior year abroad at The University of Kent at Canterbury, which was about an hour from London.

I'd spent the better part of my first two years at Mount Holyoke College working towards this moment, and I'd been fascinated with all things English since I was a young girl. When my best friend Kim and I were 10, we used to play what we called "The Rose and Georgina game." We'd affect British accents – or what seemed a pretty convincing version to us at the time – and we'd transform ourselves into two English school girls named Rose and Georgina.

We hobnobbed with royalty and enjoyed busy social calendars that included balls, operas, fox hunts, and teas. We attended a posh boarding school, but when we were home, we had maids, valets, governesses, and butlers at our beck and call.

Say what?
Brit/Yank Translator

Posh: *high-class*

The Rose and Georgina game was fun, but it was make-believe. When I got to junior high school, I had the opportunity to become pen pals with a real, live English girl named Rosalind. During our frequent correspondence, we'd gotten to know each other well; when I was 15, I'd even spent four weeks in England staying with Rosalind and her family. It was so much fun that I had vowed I'd return and live there someday.

But now that "someday" was here at last, I was utterly terrified. I stared dumbly as my fellow passengers began to gather their things and make their way off the plane. What if the coming year wasn't everything I hoped it would be? Would it be hard to make English friends? I didn't want to come all the way over here and just hang out with Americans. We'd been told that the English were not nearly as initially outgoing as American students were.

And what if I didn't like my professors? That was a worry, too. On a positive note, however, I was pretty sure I'd be happy with the English literature classes I had picked. After all, England, and Canterbury in particular, was an English major's dream. Chaucer, Dickens, Virginia Woolf, Jane Austen, Wordsworth, and Christopher Marlowe had either lived in, visited, or written about Canterbury at some point in their lives. And that was just the tip of the literary iceberg.

I had no illusions about UKC, as it was more commonly known back then, being an oasis of ivy-clad, ancient mini-castles like Oxford and Cambridge: UKC was one of the "new universities" that sprung up like so many mushrooms all over the United Kingdom in the 1960s. The building style was decidedly plate glass and concrete, but despite its less-than-inspiring architecture, it was considered one of the top universities in England.

I was more than a little nervous about the food, too. Let's be honest: in the mid 1980s the British were not famous for their culinary talents. This was before chefs like Jamie Oliver and Gordon Ramsay became the rock stars that they are now. Back at Mount Holyoke, I knew I was spoiled with the gourmet fare in our dorms' dining halls. Likewise with my mom's fabulous Italian cooking. This would definitely be the year of eating dangerously.

But as I got off the plane and stumbled through baggage claim, customs, and passport control, my most immediate concern was getting myself from London to Canterbury in one piece. I'd never traveled anywhere in a foreign country by myself. On my first trip to England in the summer of 1982, I'd been met by Rosalind and her family at the airport and had spent the next four weeks under their careful watch. This time I was completely on my own. There was no welcoming committee waiting to shepherd all of us clueless Americans through Gatwick. There was, luckily, a coach that the university had arranged for us to catch from the airport.

Say what?
Brit/Yank Translator

Coach: *a Greyhound or Peter Pan bus*

The ride from London to Canterbury was a blur – despite my combination of excitement and nerves, the jet lag won, and I slept through most of the journey. I only woke up as the coach entered the city of Canterbury and began the long climb up the hill at the top of which the university sat.

My initial impression as I got off the coach was that the place actually seemed kind of small for a university – in my mind, that word conjured up images of places like the University of Massachusetts at Amherst, which were more like cities in their own right. The overall campus didn't seem that much bigger than Mount Holyoke's. I was relieved. I was definitely a small-town, small-college person, and Mount Holyoke's student body in 1986 was not quite 2,000. UKC's almost 8,000 students seemed huge in comparison.

We must have looked like a sorry bunch as we struggled with our suitcases and assembled in front of Keynes College – one of four buildings that served as a combination of residence hall, classrooms, professor's offices, and dining hall. Keynes would be my home for the coming school year. Seemingly out of nowhere, an English student appeared at my side. He was neatly dressed in a crewneck sweater, slacks, and sensible shoes, and sported wire-rimmed eyeglasses. He had a reassuring air of competence and organization, and was clearly on the orientation committee.

"Hello, my name's Cyrus," he announced. "Let me help you with your bags. Which study bedroom are you in?"

Say what?
Brit/Yank Translator

Bags: *suitcases*

I immediately scrambled for the welcome packet I'd received the month before I left America. It contained all of the information I'd need to get settled in: confirmation of the classes I'd picked, along with my professors' names; the locations of all four of my classes; my college and dorm room assignment; UKC's academic calendar.

"Uh, it says I'm in room G2-2," I stammered. I had visions of a cell block in a prison ward.

"Great!" he chirped. "Follow me." We walked through what appeared to be Keynes's main entrance and into a large, bright, high-ceilinged lobby. In one corner of the lobby was a small, glassed-in office staffed by an official-looking older man who wore a uniform and waved at Cyrus. After stepping into the office and chatting briefly with the older man, Cyrus emerged holding a little manila envelope, which he handed to me.

"This is the key to your study bedroom," he said gravely. "Don't lose it or you'll have to pay to get a replacement." I nodded and immediately stuck the envelope in my welcome packet.

Opposite the office was a huge bulletin board that covered the lower half of the wall. The board was divided into 26 squares – one for each letter of the alphabet. Each square's corresponding alphabet letter was conspicuously posted in the middle of its square. Pinned neatly with thumbtacks (all of them white) on some of the squares were identical pieces of blue paper about the size of index cards.

"That's the Porter's Urgent Notice Board," Cyrus explained as he followed my gaze. When he could see that I had no idea what he was talking about, he elaborated. "The Porter's Urgent Notice Board is where the porters will post important notes for you from your professors. If there's an emergency at home and your family needs to reach you, that's where you'll find those messages, too. Each square has a large letter in the middle, see? Look for the letter that your surname begins with to find your message. You'll want to make sure you check your square every day."

Say what? Brit/Yank Translator	**Surname**: *last name*

6

I was unprepared for this — it seemed incredibly old-fashioned. At Mount Holyoke, many of us had phones in our dorm rooms. Those students who didn't used the hall phones that were tucked into little cubicles on every floor of our dorms. "What's a porter?" I asked stupidly.

"Oh, they're sort of property managers and security guards rolled into one," Cyrus replied. By this time I'd made the connection that the man in the glassed-in office was a porter.

We walked a little further into the lobby. "Here you'll find the Student Urgent Notice Board," Cyrus continued. He pointed to a second, slightly smaller, bulletin board with the same grid of alphabetized squares that made up the Porter's Urgent Notice Board. But instead of the tidy index cards containing messages written in what I assumed was the porter's impeccable penmanship, the Student Urgent Notice Board was plastered with a motley collection of scrawled notes on whatever piece of paper students had fished out of their pockets or day packs.

"This is where students can leave messages for each other," Cyrus noted. The ubiquitous white boards and felt-tip markers we all had hanging on the front doors of our dorm rooms back at Mount Holyoke hadn't caught on yet over here. I made a mental note to have my mom mail one to me ASAP.

From the lobby we turned left down a long corridor and past a modern staircase with open-backed stairs. Cyrus pointed at it. "Up the stairs is the dining hall — all four of the colleges have their own, but you can eat your meals in any of them."

Cyrus pushed through a set of double doors marked with a sticker that read "Fire doors — keep closed." We emerged on the other side into a large, grassy square — it was surrounded

7

on all four sides by weathered concrete walls four stories high. *Oh God,* I thought, as I looked up – *it really does look like a prison yard.* "G block is just in front of us," Cyrus said. "That's where your room is. G2-2 means you're in G block, second floor, room 2. Let's get your bags up the stairs so you can settle in."

G Block, Keynes College. Harvard Yard, it's not.

There were no elevators, like in the dorms at Mount Holyoke. The buildings here were good old-fashioned walkups. As we wrestled with my suitcases, I was glad that I hadn't over packed. At least I'd get some extra exercise every day by climbing a couple of flights of stairs.

Say what?
Brit/Yank Translator

When the English say you're on the second floor, you're actually on the third. That's because their "ground floor" is what we call the "first floor" in America.

At the top of the last flight of stairs, we pushed through another set of fire doors – I'd soon discover that the English had a preoccupation with fire doors in their public buildings – and stepped into a bright kitchenette area. There were plenty of cupboard spaces and countertops and a shiny, new, double-burner hotplate. A pizzeria-style booth was bolted to the floor. Things were looking up: I'd be able to make myself some tea or hot snacks as soon as I went shopping in Canterbury.

We walked across the kitchenette (and through yet another fire door) and along a well-lit corridor. "Ah, here we are – G2-2," Cyrus said, stopping halfway down on the right. He waited for me to find my key and unlock the door, and then we pulled my suitcases in.

I wasn't prepared for the bleakness of my study bedroom. The undecorated walls looked like cinder blocks that were painted pasty white. A twin bed covered with a brown and grey striped institutional-looking bedspread was tucked into the far corner of the room opposite a desk, chair, and bulletin board. Immediately to the right of the door were some bookshelves and a fairly large wardrobe that served as a closet.

The one window in the room was nice and big, but it was framed by a pair of panels that seemed to be cut from the same bolt of fabric as the itchy-looking bedspread. The floor featured a wall-to-wall, dark brown indoor/outdoor carpet. A single overhead light fixture hung from the middle of the ceiling. The overall effect was thoroughly depressing – to my mental shopping list I now added a desk lamp, bright bedspread, and lots of posters.

"Well, I'll leave you now so that you can unpack and make yourself at home," Cyrus announced. He must've seen the look of despair on my face, because he added, "Don't worry – a nice colorful duvet and some posters will make it look much better. Come find me at dinner tonight if you like – the doors to the dining hall open at 5:30 and they serve until 7. Welcome to UKC!" With that, he turned on his heel and left me alone in my room.

Say what?
Brit/Yank Translator

Duvet: *like a giant pillowcase into which you stuff a lightweight quilt. The pillowcase part is machine-washable.*

I put my bulging suitcases on my bed and opened them up. I had somehow managed to cram an entire school year's worth of clothing and other essential items into two large suitcases and a carry-on bag. This was no mean feat for me – I was a notorious over packer, but I'd been warned to travel light. In my sophomore year at Mount Holyoke, I'd become friendly with a senior named Allison who'd just returned from her junior year abroad at UKC. She'd been a huge help in getting me prepared, and she'd even arranged for one of her English friends who was still a student here to come look me up once I'd arrived in Canterbury.

But right now, even Allison's thoughtful advice and my months of preparation weren't helping. I was exhausted from the overnight flight to London and felt very much like a fish out of water on this new campus. Now that I was here, in my spartan room, the freak-out factor of what I'd embarked upon hit me full force.

I was alone in a foreign country – my pen pal Rosalind and her family were more than two hours away by train. There were 3,000 miles and an ocean between me and my family, friends, and boyfriend. We had all decided before I left that I would not be flying back to the States for Christmas, so this would be the first one I wouldn't be spending with my close-knit family. Nothing here was familiar, and it all seemed suddenly overwhelming. I began to wonder if I'd made a terrible mistake.

Naturally, I did what any self-respecting, sheltered, female American college student would've done in my situation: I sat down on the floor and burst into tears.

In case you don't have your own Allison, here are some things to consider while you're still Stateside:

Pack light. Throw everything you want to take abroad into a big pile on your bed. Now cut the pile in half. Then do it again. Trust me on this one: you're going to accumulate a lot of new stuff while you're away.

Get a medical and dental checkup and make sure your vaccinations are up to date. The last thing you want to do on your year abroad is navigate the complexities of your host country's healthcare system. You can't plan for emergencies, of course, but take care of any little health problems or conditions while you're still in the United States. That way they won't turn into big crises when you're thousands of miles away from home.

Make two copies of your passport. Take one copy with you and keep it in a separate (safe) place from your original passport. Leave the other copy at home. Passports can get lost or stolen just like anything else, and having a copy on hand will speed the replacement process. And while we're on the subject, make sure that your passport is valid for at least six months beyond the end of your year abroad.

Organize your finances. How much money will you need during your year away? What kind of traveling do you plan to do on weekends and at term breaks? Make sure to allow for a social life. Put together some kind of budget before you leave. You might even be able to open a bank account in your host country before you arrive there.

Chapter Two

I'm not sure how long I sat there crying, but after a while I heard a soft knock at my door.

"Uh...who is it?" I asked as I got off the floor, hurried to the mirror on the side of the wardrobe, and tried to make myself as presentable as possible.

"Diane, it's Colin – Allison's friend," a male voice answered in an English accent. "I've come to introduce myself and check that you've arrived safely."

I don't think I was ever so happy to hear another human being's voice. Here was a connection, however tenuous, to my life back in America.

"Please, come in, Colin," I said as I opened the door. "I'm afraid you've caught me feeling a little sorry for myself. Allison told me so much about you – it's nice to finally meet you in person."

Colin looked a little worried when he saw my red face and puffy eyes. "Oh, if I've chosen a bad time, I'll come back later. I just thought you might like..."

"No, you're not interrupting at all – the pity party is officially over," I said as I attempted what I hoped was a convincing laugh. "Please, have a seat." I pulled my desk chair across the floor for Colin and sat down between my suitcases on the bed.

"Did you have a good journey?" he asked politely.

"Oh yes, thanks – nothing really exciting. It was long and tiring. I feel like I could sleep for two days."

"I hope you don't think I'm being presumptuous, Diane, but perhaps you'd be better off staying awake," Colin suggested.

"I'd be happy to take you on a tour of the campus. Then we can have some lunch. If you're up for it, we can head down to a pub after dinner this evening for a quick drink. If that's all right with you, of course."

He seemed afraid that he'd overstepped his boundaries. After all, he'd only just met me, and here he was planning out the rest of my day and evening. Instead of being annoyed or offended, however, I was incredibly grateful that Allison had anticipated how overwhelmed and lost I'd feel right after arriving.

"Colin, that sounds terrific – it sure beats sitting here in this room. Let's go." I grabbed my welcome packet and we set off.

"Allison told me you were an English and French literature major," Colin said as we made our way to the Keynes lobby. "I'll be taking my degree in American Studies. Did she tell you that I spent last year in America, studying in Indiana?"

"Yes, she did. Was it a good year? I'll bet you're glad to be back home in England, though."

"It was a smashing experience. I missed everyone in England while I studied in the States, of course, but I really settled in well in America. To be quite honest with you, I've found that it's been a bit difficult getting used to things back here. I was really pleased when Allison told me you'd be coming – it will be lovely to be around another Mount Holyoke student again."

As we walked around campus, I realized that although the architecture wasn't particularly impressive, the university's location was. The entire campus was at the top of a high hill – below it sat the skyline of Canterbury, which was dominated by its enormous cathedral. The cathedral seemed to loom over all of the streets and the tiled rooftops, and even though we were looking down upon it, the effect was breathtaking.

"It's beautiful, isn't it?" Colin asked as he watched me take in the view. "I never get tired of looking at it. Wait until the Christmas season – the cathedral is lit up every night. It looks as if it's floating over the city."

UKC's campus, as I'd first suspected, was surprisingly compact. Colin showed me around the four major colleges (Keynes, Eliot, Rutherford, and Darwin), plus the library, a computing lab, a sports complex, a theatre/drama building, and finally, the Registry. This last building, Colin explained, was the university's administrative center.

"Oh, the Registry! That's where the American and other foreign students are supposed to pick up their mail every day," I said as we approached the building. "Are there that many of us that we need our own special place to get our mail?"

"Actually, about a fifth of UKC's students come from outside the U.K.," Colin answered. "And nearly half of those are from America. We have quite a diverse population, I think you'll find." In the coming days, I'd meet students from the U.K., the U.S., Sri Lanka, India, Iraq, Indonesia, Singapore, Japan, China, Canada, Israel, France, Greece, Cyprus, Pakistan, and even Argentina. The university was a mini United Nations.

"Have you met any of the other people on your corridor yet?" Colin asked as we continued our tour.

"Not officially. Some of the people who were with me on the coach from Gatwick got off in front of Keynes with me. I think a

15

few of them might be on my floor, because I heard doors slamming down the hall. And I know there are four other Mount Holyoke students here."

"Oh, well, that's lovely – it'll be good for you to have some familiar faces here in case you get homesick."

"No way!" I snapped. "I didn't come 3,000 miles to hang out with people from Mount Holyoke! If I'd wanted to do that, I would've just stayed home. I want to make British friends." I stopped ranting when I saw Colin's expression. His eyes widened and before I could decide whether he was angry or surprised, he threw his head back and burst into laughter.

"Ah, you sound just like Allison did when she arrived for her junior year abroad here," he said, grinning. "She told me I wouldn't have to worry about wondering what was on your mind, Diane. That's one of the things I love most about you Yanks – you're refreshingly blunt. Unlike us Brits with our stiff upper lip."

Actually, I was beginning to think that Colin was refreshingly blunt himself. He wasn't at all how I imagined a typical Englishman to be: reserved, cool, aloof. He seemed to read my mind, because he said, "I'm probably not what you expected as far as a model English person."

"Oh, most definitely not. I don't see a tweed cape on you, or Wellington boots, and there's no hunting dog trotting along by your side," I joked. "However, you are way more polite than any American guy I've ever met. Now tell me the truth – what's the food really like here? Is it awful? Will I need to have my parents mail all kinds of care packages to me?"

"Well, it's definitely not your mum's cooking, and it's not

16

going to win any Michelin stars, if that's what you're asking," Colin confirmed. "Allison used to tell me the most wonderful stories about your famous Mount Holyoke Sunday brunches and the omelet stations. You won't find those here. But it's not too bad, overall. Lots of chips – with everything, except at breakfast. And gravy – we're mad keen on gravy over here."

Say what?
Brit/Yank Translator

Michelin stars: *A rating system for top-notch restaurants. So named because you'll find them in the authoritative Michelin guides that discerning European travelers use to plan their vacations.*

Chips: *French fries*

Mad keen on: *to be crazy about*

"Except at breakfast, I hope."

"No – no gravy at breakfast. We do have kippers, though."

"Those nasty fish? Oh, yuk – I think I'll pass. You don't really eat those, do you?"

"No, I don't, but lots of people do. Was that the right answer?"

"Yes, thanks. We can still be friends," I said.

"Well, I don't know about you, but I'm ready for lunch after all this walking," Colin said. "What do you say we throw you right to UKC's culinary wolves? Did you bring your meal plan card with you? You can use it at any of the four colleges' dining halls."

I panicked momentarily – just about everything of importance was in the welcome packet I'd been carrying since our walk began. I remembered selecting a meal plan in the summer, when I'd mailed off all of my registration materials. I hadn't given it a further thought since then. *The card has to be here somewhere*, I thought, as I quickly rifled through the packet.

"Um…police registration form, class schedule, student handbook, campus map…oh wait! Here it is!" I announced.

"You'll want to keep that in a safe place – it's a right pain in the backside to get it replaced. Let's see – we're nearest Eliot College right now. Let's go there."

Inside the dining hall, Colin frowned. "What a queue," he said as he handed me a tray. "All for a beefburger and some chips." I was starting to wonder if the student handbook in my welcome packet included a handy British English-American English translator[1]. When I stayed with Rosalind and her family back in 1982, I was the source of much amusement when I used American slang.

The lunch wasn't bad, but I could see that if I had a beefburger and chips every day, I'd gain way more than the

---

Say what?

Brit/Yank Translator

Queue: *a line. It also refers to the act of "lining up." You join a queue to wait for a bus, for example, or you can queue for a train ticket.*
Beefburger: *a hamburger*

---

[1] It didn't. Which is why I'm doing it here.

18

dreaded Freshman Ten I'd put on at Mount Holyoke. While we ate, Colin told me a little about his family. He had one younger sister and had grown up in a town just outside Liverpool.

"Liverpool?! Allison never told me that," I said. "I'm a huge Beatles fan – have you done the whole Beatles tour thing? Have you visited the Cavern Club? Can you tour the Quarry School, or John's Aunt Mimi's house?"

Colin laughed. "No, I'm afraid not – and I hate to disappoint you, but you do know that the Cavern Club doesn't exist anymore? There's a car park there now. But I'll tell you what: come and visit during term break and we'll do the touristy Beatles excursions, all right?" That sounded like a perfect plan to me.

Say what?
Brit/Yank Translator

Car park: *parking lot*

I decided that Colin must've been a tour guide in a past life. After lunch, he continued to show me around campus. When we stopped in front of the university's shop, he explained, "Now here is where you'll be spending a lot of time. It's where you can pick up all kinds of supplies you'll need for your classes – you know, notebooks, pens, and the like. There's a small post office here, too, where you can post all your letters home. This is also where the university's bank branch and cash point are. You can open your deposit account and your current account before classes start."

Cash point: ATM
Deposit account: *savings account*
Current account: *checking account*

It seemed that most college students in the U.K. were apparently just like their American counterparts in their inability to manage their money; Colin explained that your cash point card would only allow you to withdraw a certain amount of cash every week. Once you hit the limit, that was it. You'd have to wait until the following week started to get more.

I'd arrived at UKC armed with a stash of traveler's checks and about 200 dollars' worth of British pounds to get me through my first few weeks. My parents would transfer the rest of my summer-job earnings from home once I got my bank accounts set up over here.

By now I was feeling a lot less nervous and much more excited about meeting some more students and exploring Canterbury itself. My welcome packet promised a busy first week for the "international students" that would be filled with all of the usual boring things, like orientation meetings, but fun things like specially arranged visits to Canterbury Cathedral and Leeds Castle. For the rest of today and tonight, though, we were pretty much on our own and free to unpack and relax.

As Colin and I headed back across campus to Keynes College, he said, "Well, that about ends the grand tour, I reckon. I'm sure you want to unpack all of your bags. Why don't I come back to your room around 5:45 or so to collect you for dinner this evening?"

"Sounds like you're arranging to pick up some boxes or packages at a loading dock."

"Well, what sounds better to you?"

"I don't know. How about you'll just come 'get' me? Sounds less stuffy."

"You mean less British."

"I never said that."

Colin grinned. "I'll come get you at 5:45, then."

Say what?
Brit/Yank Translator

Collect: *get; pick up*

Once again I was alone in my dorm room. I still hadn't taken a single thing out of my suitcases and I felt like I could use a long, hot shower. But I really wanted to meet some more students and find out who else was in G block. When Colin and I had come back upstairs to my room after our walk around campus, we had heard some voices and seen some study bedroom doors ajar. It was time to meet the neighbors.

Know Before You Go

Minimizing Jet Lag

We've put men on the moon and eradicated polio, but so far nobody's figured out how to prevent jet lag. Caffeine and alcohol can make it even worse, so avoid these on your overseas flight.

When I spent my junior year abroad, most flights out of the U.S. and into Europe were overnight. That meant you arrived at your destination at the crack of dawn local time the following morning. Nowadays, it's a lot easier to find overseas flights that leave the U.S. in the morning and arrive in Europe in the evening.

Whichever option you choose to fly overseas, do yourself a huge favor and stay awake once you arrive in your host country; then turn in for the evening when the locals do. You'll minimize jet lag and get adjusted to your new time zone a whole lot faster.

✧ Chapter Three ✧

My own floor seemed like a good place to start, so I just began knocking on doors and introducing myself. At the far end of the hall I met Sara, a tall, shy American junior year abroad student from Indiana University; I recognized her from the bus ride out of Gatwick. Directly across the hall was Sharon, a blond English girl from Nottingham who seemed like an earthy-crunchy type.

Next door to me was Rika, a slender Japanese girl who was here on an exchange year as well. There was also a Chinese student who said her name so quickly that I promptly forgot it and was too embarrassed to ask her to repeat it every time we saw each other after that. And finally there was Amy, a graceful American dance student who had the most beautiful hair I'd ever seen.

Heading back towards my room, I realized that my corridor was cut in half by still another pair of fire doors. On the other side, I met a couple of English girls, a Greek Cypriot girl, and Julie, a fellow American whose home college was UC San Diego. Nobody else seemed to be home on this half of the corridor, so I went downstairs to the floor below me.

The first door I knocked on was answered by an American named Kathy, who was a physics student from UMass Amherst. When I told her that I went to Mount Holyoke, which was only about 15 minutes away, we spent the next half hour talking about home. What's more, she grew up on Cape Cod, in a town near Dennisport, where my family had vacationed every summer since as far back as I could remember.

"I met some really nice English students as I was moving in

this morning," Kathy said. "One's in the room right across from me. Let's see if she's in." We went across the hall to a room whose door was wide open and from which several voices spilled out. "Oh good – they're all in there. Come on, I'll introduce you." She walked right in without knocking. "Arvine – here's another American for you to meet. This is Diane – she's from a college right near mine."

Everyone in the room stopped talking and turned around to look at Kathy and me standing in the doorway. I immediately felt awkward – like I was in one of those cheesy westerns where the stranger in town walks into the saloon and everyone stops what they're doing and just stares. Luckily, this scene went a lot better and didn't end with a bar brawl or a gunfight.

A young woman got up from where she was sitting and walked over to us. She was tall, wore glasses with large frames, and had enormous brown eyes. "Hi, I'm Arvine," she said in a soft voice. "It's lovely to meet you." Then she did something that was decidedly un-English: she bent down and gave me a long hug.

"She did that when I met her, too," Kathy said, laughing. "Not what you were expecting, huh?"

"No, definitely not!" I answered. "Although I come from a big Italian family where we all hug each other. So you'd be right at home with my relatives, Arvine. That's a really pretty name. Where does it come from?"

"Thank you –my parents thought it up themselves."

Arvine took my hand and led me over to meet the rest of her friends: Jeremy, who had a shock of black hair and was all arms and legs; stocky, clean-cut Hugh, who was born to English parents but grew up in Zambia; and Ben, a bespectacled, quiet guy who had what the British call a "double-barreled" surname – making it quite likely that he came from money.

Say what?
Brit/Yank Translator

Double-barreled:
hyphenated

"So are you all first-year students?" I asked them.

"Oh no – we're third-years," Arvine answered.

"Third-years? So that means you'll be graduating in the cathedral!" I'd seen photos of the ceremony in the UKC viewbook. We'd been told that unlike American college students, most English students are at university for just three years, unless they take a year out at a university abroad. In that case, they have to come back to their home university in England for a fourth and final year before they can graduate.

"Yes, we're really looking forward to it," Arvine replied.

Kathy and I stayed and visited with Arvine and her friends for a while. We all talked about what we'd be studying during the coming year, and which degrees they would be taking. Hugh entertained us with stories about his Zambian childhood spent running barefoot along the banks of the Zambezi River. He talked about giraffes and zebras as if they were as common as chipmunks.

"I even saw a pig fly, once," he remarked casually.

At this, Arvine started to giggle. "Oh no, Hugh, you're not going to tell that story to these poor girls." Jeremy and Ben groaned.

"As a matter of fact, I am," Hugh said. "So, you know that saying 'when pigs fly'? Meaning it's something that's never going to happen? Well, there I am playing with a bunch of my school mates by the Zambezi. It was a really gorgeous, sunny day and suddenly we hear a huge commotion and all this squealing. Some people nearby kept pigs, so we didn't think much about the noise at first.

"Suddenly the squealing began to sound like it was above us. Then one of my mates points and yells, 'look up in the sky!' Well bless me — a bloody great eagle had just swooped down and caught one of the piglets for his dinner! That piglet dangled from the eagle's talons, squealing away." At this point, Hugh performed an impressive re-enactment of said piglet dangling and squealing. "The eagle flew away with it and disappeared. So there you have it. Pigs can indeed fly. And I saw it happen."

Kathy and I were speechless — then we started laughing so hard that we began snorting, which set Arvine, Jeremy, Hugh, and Ben to laughing at us. By the time we stopped, we all had tears running down our cheeks and were gasping for air.

"Well, with that visual in my mind, I'm going to head back to my room and start unpacking my suitcases," I said. "Thanks for a really fun visit!" Before we left, Arvine and her friends invited Kathy and me to come out to a local pub with them on the following night.

"It's a proper country pub not far from the university," Arvine told us. "It's not studenty at all. We found it during our first year."

"What do you think?" I asked Kathy, who nodded yes. "Sounds good — what time should we go?"

"We'll come collect you in Kathy's room after dinner tomorrow," Jeremy replied. There was that word "collect" again.

"O.K., see you then!" Kathy and I headed off to our rooms.

I wish I could say that after hanging out with Kathy, Arvine, and all of her friends, I got straight to work unpacking and making my room a little more homey. But I'm a terrible procrastinator, so the prospect of a shower was much more appealing now. I gathered all my bathroom things and some clothes, headed down the hall, and walked straight into another reminder of how spoiled I was at home.

Back at Mount Holyoke, our dorms had a huge bathroom on each floor. There were at least four shower stalls (each with its own separate dressing area) to a bathroom, as well as four or five toilet cubicles. In addition to that, there was a bank of sinks and a series of cubbyholes mounted to the wall where we could keep our bathroom caddies so we didn't have to keep lugging them back and forth from our dorm rooms to the bathroom.

But here was what my mom would call a rude awakening. One not-very-large bathroom served the eight women on my half of the corridor. Directly in front of me was a shower room with a door that locked from the inside and a changing area. Next to that was an even smaller room with a toilet – again, the door was lockable from inside. Opposite these was a mirror that was mounted to the wall, with a little sink under it.

To my horror, the taps on the sink were exactly like the ones in my pen pal Rosalind's house – with separate faucets for the hot and cold water. I remembered alternately scalding or freezing my face several times on that first trip to England until

I'd finally gotten the hang of making a little bowl with my washcloth in my hands and putting it first under the hot tap and then under the cold one.

The main door I'd just come through was made of tempered glass that was blurred for privacy and was not lockable from the inside, so at least that meant that three different people could be in here at the same time. It could've been worse, I supposed. I sighed, stepped into the shower room, locked the door, and turned on the water.

I felt much better after my shower. On my way out of the bathroom, I noticed another tempered glass door right next to it. To my surprise, this contained a similar room, except that instead of a shower room, this had a bathtub, a sink, and a little toilet cubicle that was tucked into the corner.

I recalled how much Rosalind and her family loved their baths, and this seemed pretty representative of the English in general. Personally, I hate baths. I never feel clean after one. Here was one room I would most definitely not be using in the coming year.

Back in my bedroom, I was now ready to empty out the suitcases and get to work. Because Allison warned me to pack light, I didn't really have a whole lot of things to put away. She jokingly told me that once she got back to the States, she never wore her "junior year abroad" clothes again – she'd just worn them so damn much in England that she was sick of them.

It really had been a challenge to pack clothes for an entire school year. I wouldn't have the luxury of going home to my parents' house for the weekend and carting more stuff back to college with me every time, like I was used to doing at Mount Holyoke. And I didn't want to bother my parents with the expense of mailing stuff overseas to me. I also assumed I might be buying the odd thing or two here in England. I started lifting things out of the cases and trying to organize them more or less by season.

I'd made sure I'd packed all my favorites – I figured if I was going to be wearing the same clothes a lot, I'd better love them. I'd brought enough clothes to last me through a week or so in each season before I had to do laundry. And that was something else I had to find out about – where the laundry room was in Keynes.

In addition to my clothes, I'd brought along a few things from home to decorate my dorm room. I had a small poster of the United Kingdom to put on my wall; Allison said it was a great conversation-starter with the English students, because they'd show you the town they came from. You could also use it to plan your sightseeing trips. But of course I didn't have any tape, so for now I just tacked the map to my bulletin board.

Up on the bookshelves went a few of my favorite novels and some framed photos of my parents and sisters, as well as one of me and my best friend Kim. I had one of my boyfriend Sal, too, but I hesitated to put that out, which made me feel kind of guilty. I probably should've broken up with him before I'd left for England – in fact, I knew I should've broken up with him before I left for England.

I worried that having someone back in the States would distract me while I was having all sorts of fun in England. I wanted to be completely present in this incredible year that I'd

worked so hard to earn. And it also didn't seem fair to expect
Sal to just sit there back in Massachusetts and wait for me. We
hadn't even talked about him coming to visit me while I was
studying abroad.

To say that things with Sal were a little complicated was an
understatement. We'd only started dating a little over four
months ago, when we'd met at my summer job. He was older
than I was. Okay, full disclosure: he was WAY older than I was,
by more than 10 years. My parents nearly had heart attacks
when I told them, but they didn't forbid me to see him. I think
that knowing I'd be gone in October for 10 months made it a
summer fling, in their eyes.

And if I was being completely honest with myself, I'd admit
the same thing. Sal's feelings for me were clearly stronger than
mine were for him. I think that I just got swept off my feet and
carried away by the whole idea of a sophisticated, older man.
When I went on dates with him, I was in a whole new world
where I was introduced to music I'd never heard before and
gourmet restaurants I would never have been able to afford
on my own.

He had a prestigious job – at least it seemed so in my
20-year-old eyes. Dating him was exciting and different, but we
were in two completely different phases of life and moving in
opposite directions. When we'd said goodbye at Logan Airport,
we'd agreed to let the coming year play out. I looked down at
his photo sitting in my hands and put it in the back of one of my
desk drawers.

The last things I unpacked were my Sony Walkman and my
favorite cassette tapes from home. Next to books, I am most

passionate about music. Back at Mount Holyoke, I was an FCC-licensed DJ on the college's radio station. If you really wanted to torture me, all you'd have to do is put me alone in a room with nothing to read and no music to listen to. In the mid '80s, CDs had only just come on the scene. As much as I loved music, I was an impoverished college student on financial aid whose meager funds made such extravagances impossible. The money I'd saved during my summer job was going to subsidize my social life over here and enable me to travel. CDs and a CD player would have to wait until I got home to America, graduated from Mount Holyoke, and got my first real job.

When I was done unpacking, I stood with my back to my single window, looked around, and surveyed the results of my work. My dorm room was...still looking like a prison cell, only there was slightly more stuff on the shelves and in the closet. A shopping trip into Canterbury was definitely in order – maybe I could go exploring before classes started up.

I looked at my watch; it was almost 5:45. Where had the day gone? Colin would be here any minute. Maybe Kathy would like to join us for dinner, too. I ran downstairs and banged on her door.

"Hey! Are you headed over to dinner? Want to join me?" I asked as soon as she opened up. From the state of her room, I could see that Kathy had been unpacking too, and had been about as successful in "transforming" her room as I'd been.

"Sure – I was just coming up to see you. Arvine and her friends headed out a while ago, but I wasn't ready. We'll see them tomorrow night, anyway."

"Colin's coming with us – he's this English guy I met through one of my Mount Holyoke friends at home. He said he'll take me down to one of the local pubs in Canterbury after dinner if I'm still awake. Want to come? It'll be fun, and that way it won't seem like a date." I didn't want to be sending the wrong message to my new friend – apparently American girls had a reputation over here for being "fast."

Colin was just arriving at my room when Kathy and I pushed through the fire doors at the top of the stairs. "Hello," he said. "Ready to experience your first UKC dinner? You seem to have survived the lunch all right."

"Hey Colin! Would you mind if a friend came along? This is Kathy – she's from Massachusetts too. She's from UMass, near Mount Holyoke."

"It's a pleasure to meet you, Kathy," Colin said as he shook her hand. "I'm afraid that you missed my guided tour of campus today, but Diane and I will be going on a good old-fashioned pub crawl this evening if you'd like to come along."

Know Before You Go

If you are studying abroad in the U.K., you will soon become familiar with the pub crawl. Here's how it works: you and your friends have a drink (or three) in as many pubs as you can in one night before last call. You walk to the pubs, so nobody has to drive. By the time you get to the final pub, you're likely stumbling, staggering, or crawling. Hence the name.

Here was an English phrase that was new to Kathy and me. "A pub crawl? What the hell is that?" I asked.

"I'm only joking," Colin said reassuringly. "Since you've just arrived in England today, we'll visit one pub this evening and work our way up to a full-on pub crawl later."

"And what does the typical English student drink at the pubs, Colin?" I questioned as we headed over to the dining hall. On my first visit to England in 1982, I'd been too young to drink. Now that I was legal, I didn't want to order something lame and look like a dumb tourist.

"Well, lager is pretty popular if you're used to drinking beer at home. If beer isn't your sort of thing, then you might like the cider – except our cider over here is alcoholic. Those are the cheapest things to drink on a student budget."

We crossed the quad, entered the lobby area of Keynes, and climbed the stairs to the Keynes dining hall. The familiar sounds of silverware clinking on plates, chairs being pushed in and pulled out, and multiple conversations greeted us. Some things are universal. I could already smell the chips – it was going to be tough trying to stay away from them at every single lunch and dinner!

The Keynes dining hall was massive and filled with long, banquet-style tables that were set up in parallel rows (think Hogwarts). The entire space was divided into two halves by a wide "aisle" that ran down the middle of the dining hall. To get into the food queue and pick up your meals, you had to walk down this aisle – giving everyone who was already sitting down ample opportunity to check you out. It had the disconcerting effect of making you feel as if you were running a gauntlet or walking down a fashion show runway.

As Kathy, Colin, and I walked down to join the queue, I prayed to God that I wouldn't do something completely idiotic, like tripping and falling flat on my face. Just before we got into the queue, I noticed several rolling carts against the wall that were at least six feet high. They had rows upon rows of narrow shelves, where students could slide in their meal trays when they were finished eating. A gangly-looking student approached the cart and quickly slid his tray in. As he turned to walk away, an almighty crash filled the air – plates smashed, glasses shattered, and silverware clattered to the floor.

"Hooraaaaaaaaaaaaaaaay," a group of nearby guys cheered sarcastically, much to the humiliation of the poor student, who tried to make as inconspicuous an exit as possible. One of the kitchen staff, red-faced and clearly annoyed, immediately appeared on the scene and started clearing the mess up.

"First-year," Colin commented to us, as the offending student quickly beat it out of the dining hall. "Those rolling carts that you put your meal trays on when you're done eating? Fair warning: they don't have backs. Watch that you don't push another

An infamous rolling cart, waiting for its next unsuspecting victim.

tray all the way out the opposite end and onto the floor. If you make a really spectacular mess, you'll get cheers AND applause."

We joined the long line and presented our meal plan cards for inspection. The food looked like the usual institutional fare, but there was a pretty wide selection. About a half-dozen kitchen staff were stationed behind the food line serving up the night's offerings. One lady was particularly intimidating – she looked as if she'd been dropped into the kitchen straight out of the 1950s, with horn-rimmed glasses, teased hair that was threatening to burst out of her hair net, and electric blue eye shadow. She towered over the rest of her colleagues as she walked up and down behind them and barked out orders.

Colin whispered, "That's Mean Jean the Economy Queen. Nobody knows her real name. She's been here forever. Don't ask for second helpings, at least within her earshot, unless you want to be told off. She thinks we're still on wartime rations."

I was especially entertained by a skinny, short kitchen worker who seemed to have one sole purpose in the serving line, and he took his job very seriously. As we passed by his station, he made eye contact with me and announced "GRAVY!" at the top of his lungs, ladle poised and brimming with the greasy brown liquid that passed for institutional gravy.

"Is that a question or a statement?" I asked Colin as I withheld my tray. I didn't want to hurt Gravy Guy's feelings, but I wasn't in the mood for what he was offering.

"So Colin, which college do you live in?" I asked, as we found seats and began eating. I realized I'd never asked him when we were walking around campus earlier today.

"Oh, I'm over in Parkwood Court, the self-catering flats," he answered. "They're on the far side of campus, past the sports complex."

Say what?
Brit/Yank Translator

Flat: *apartment*

"So how come you're in a campus apartment and not in one of the colleges, like we are?" Kathy asked.

"They give first priority for the flats to third-years, or to people like me, who took their third year abroad and are coming back for the final year at university. As a first-year, you're automatically given a study bedroom in one of the four colleges. But you're on your own for your second year."

"What do you mean?" I said. "You can't get on-campus housing for your second year?" This seemed strange to me – I always thought of "tuition, room, and board" and not just "tuition." I didn't realize that it wasn't always a package deal for English students.

"No – you have to find your own lodgings for your second year." If you planned ahead and arranged your second-year accommodation before the end of your first year, Colin explained, you ended up with a decent apartment in Herne Bay or Whitstable, two seaside villages that were a short car or bus ride from campus. Both places offered lots of reasonably priced, well-maintained student flats. But if you waited too late, Colin continued, you ended up with what students referred to as a "Herne Bay horror" – a single, shabbily furnished bedroom with a shared bathroom in a run-down rooming house that had seen better days.

"Those bedsits are dead cheap, but they're dreadful," Colin said with a shudder. "The central heating is barely functional, and good luck getting hold of your landlady if anything needs repairing. And the kitchens in those places? You wouldn't want to risk cooking in them. You're better off buying a meal plan and eating at the university."

"Aren't there any apartments down in Canterbury?" I questioned. Surely there had to be nice places down the hill that a student could rent for the school year.

"Canterbury is a major tourist destination. Nobody wants to let a flat or a bedroom to a student for a pittance when they can get a far better price by converting a spare bedroom in their home to a Bed and Breakfast accommodation." It was simple economics; the tourists had more money than the students did. "When we walk down to the pub in Canterbury tonight, we'll pass lots of B+Bs."

Say what?
Brit/Yank Translator

Let: *rent*

Again I was reminded of how easy I had it at Mount Holyoke. Many of the dorms that surrounded the beautiful central "green" on campus were lovely old red-brick and ivy-covered buildings with towers, crenellations, and porches for sitting. Even the less desirable dorms on the far edges of the campus were luxurious by UKC standards. And every single student at Mount Holyoke, regardless of her year, was guaranteed a room on campus.

"So where did you live during your second year, Colin?" Kathy asked.

37

"I was lucky – my friends and I knew someone who owned a small house in a tiny village only a few minutes' drive from Canterbury. He was going to Europe for an extended business assignment and needed someone to live in the house for him. He offered us a low rent if we promised to keep up the house and the garden for him while he was away."

At this point, I was starting to wonder why Colin wasn't interested in hanging out with all of his own friends, especially since he hadn't seen them during the entire year he'd spent at Indiana University. It was really great of him to sort of adopt me, but he must have a bunch of friends he'd made at UKC that he was eager to catch up with. So I asked, "Colin, do your friends live with you at Parkwood, too?"

"Ah, that's the only downside about taking your third year out when you study at an English university. While I was having fun in the States doing a year out, most of my friends had their third year at UKC and graduated. They're in the working world now."

Kathy and I must've looked as if we felt sorry for Colin, because he quickly added, "Don't you girls worry – I've already got plans to visit them on weekends, and one is near enough to Canterbury that we can meet up for the odd pub lunch on a Sunday. And speaking of pubs, who's ready to walk into town for a drink?"

We got up, returned our trays to the carts (without incident, to my relief), and headed down to the Keynes lobby. There were lots of students milling around, reuniting with each other after the long summer, and planning the coming evening.

"Right – you know the coach you arrived on?" Colin asked

us. "See that roundabout across the road over there? Every 15 or 20 minutes, you can catch a red, double-decker coach that will take you into Canterbury. It's only a short ride and it's not that expensive – less than a pound – but if you'd rather save your money, we can walk into town."

Say what?
Brit/Yank Translator

Roundabout:
rotary; traffic circle

I was all for that – I was determined not to have to ask my parents for an emergency loan during the coming school year. Before I'd arrived in England, I had even figured out a rough budget so I'd know how much I was able to spend every week. I wanted to be completely self-sufficient, and if I could save a few pounds here and there, that was even better.

"Do you have a car, Colin?" I asked, fully expecting him to say no. None of my friends at Mount Holyoke had one, and we really didn't need a car there, since the bus system went nearly everywhere we were interested in going. It seemed like the coaches and trains here in England did a good job of getting people where they needed to go. I'd heard that the U.K.'s public transportation system was much better than America's.

"As a matter of fact, I do have a car here – but it's back at Parkwood right now. The drink-driving laws in England are pretty strict. It's not worth the risk of getting done and having your license taken away. Besides, it's nearly as far to walk from the city car parks to the pubs as it is to walk from UKC to the pubs. So, are you girls ready to walk off your dinner?"

Know Before You Go

What to Do When You Arrive (and It's Not Sleep)

As tempting as it may be to have a quick nap when you've arrived at your destination, don't. Instead, dump your suitcases in your dorm room and start knocking on doors; introduce yourself to the other people on your floor. Sure, this may be a little outside your comfort zone, but it's the fastest way to meet people and will force you to get out there.

Invite one of the people you've just met to go for a walk around campus with you. Familiarize yourselves with the buildings, find out where your classes will meet, and generally get the lay of the land. You didn't come here to hide in your room and be homesick!

✧ Chapter Four ✧

It was already dusk as we left campus and began to walk down the hill and towards the city. Our destination was The Falstaff Tap, a pub whose name conjured up in my English major's mind a Shakespearean-era, half-timbered and thatched roof building. As we walked, Colin explained to Kathy and me that you had to be careful about which pubs on the High Street you went to if you were a student.

"Some of the pubs, like The Falstaff, are quite studenty – we're welcome there. But some of them, like The Bishop's Finger across the street, don't like students at all."

"Why is that?" questioned Kathy. "A customer is a customer, right?"

"Not when that customer is a uni student. I'm afraid that a few bad seeds have given the lot of us rather a bad reputation amongst some of the pub owners. You'll be able to tell which pubs are studenty and which aren't the moment you walk in."

That made me remember something: I told Colin about how Arvine and her friends had invited Kathy and me out tomorrow night to a "non-studenty" pub – there wouldn't be trouble, would there? I didn't want to start my big year off by getting kicked out of a bar or causing an international incident. "She said it wasn't far from campus and that they kind of stumbled on it in their first year. They're third-years now," I added.

Colin smiled. "I shouldn't worry too much, Diane. I'm sure you're in capable hands with Arvine and her friends. It's mostly the pubs on the High Street where you have to pay attention."

In the daylight that remained, I took in as much of our walk as I could. We'd now left the university behind and were walking down the long hill into Canterbury itself. As exhausted as I was, I was still pretty excited. I'd slept the entire bus ride from London to Canterbury, so I'd missed all of this earlier this morning.

Pretty soon we started passing "detached" houses, as Colin called them. Each one had beautiful lawns, hedges, shrubs, and gardens, and the houses themselves were well-kept. No shabby student flats here.

As we got a little closer to the medieval Westgate, one of the old, official entrances to the city proper, the detached houses began to give way to what Colin told us were "semi-detached" houses. Each half of these houses had its own separate color scheme, the result being that one half might have royal blue trim on the windows, doors, and exterior plumbing, for example, and the other half might have hunter green. It made for a very colorful walk.

Even closer to the Westgate was a new kind of housing. "Those are terraced houses," Colin said. "That's where you'll find a lot of the B+Bs I was telling you about earlier." Sure enough, a good number of these places had neatly painted signs reading "B+B" that hung over their front doors or were placed in a prominent front window.

Say what? **Brit/Yank Translator**	**Detached house:** *single-family dwelling* **Semi-detached house:** *duplex* **Terraced house:** *row house*

Colin told us that having a B+B was a good way for home-owners to earn extra money without the hassle and expense of running a real hotel. For travelers, B+Bs were a good option, too: they were less expensive than a hotel and much nicer than a youth hostel. "If your parents come to visit you during the coming year," he said, "you might think about booking their accommodations in places like these. You can ask the owners to show you the room and decide for yourselves if your parents would like it."

This was good to know: later in the spring, my own mom and dad would be coming to England. It would be their first trip abroad in their entire lives. They'd start in London, where my dad would run the London Marathon. "So are B+Bs all over England, even in London?" I asked.

"You'll be hard-pressed to find them in central London, I'm afraid," Colin replied, "There are lots of small, family-run hotels in the capital, however. But yes – B+Bs are pretty much all over England."

"What about really fancy hotels?" Kathy asked. "There must be some four-star places here in Canterbury, right?"

"Oh, of course. That would be The County Hotel, further on down the High Street. It's very posh, indeed. It'll set you back a few bob."

Say what?
Brit/Yank Translator

Bob: *pound sterling*

We were now at Westgate, which was one of the fortified gates in the medieval walls that had once completely encircled Canterbury. When it was first built, the stone must have been beautiful, but six hundred years and, more recently, the exhaust from cars and trucks had rendered it various shades of grey and sooty black.

The "gate" part of Westgate was an enormous central arch that was just big enough for cars and buses to drive through on their way to the High Street or the London Road. Two impressive towers a couple of stories high sat atop the arch, punctuated here and there by arrow slits. Crenellations decorated the top. Something important must be up there, because set into the stone at street level was a gigantic wooden door with iron hinges and ring pulls that reminded me of something you'd see in a castle.

Westgate.

Car traffic is now re-routed around the historic tower, much to the relief of drivers and their passengers.

"What's inside?" I shouted to Colin over the noise of the traffic. Cars and trucks flew by us at a breakneck pace, and I was glad that the sidewalk curved around Westgate for pedestrians like us. Only somebody with a death wish would try to walk through that central arch.

"Do you know, in all the times I've walked past Westgate, I never once wondered that," Colin yelled back. "We'll have to find out this year. Oh, watch this," he shouted, and pointed at the traffic screaming up behind us.

To Kathy's and my astonishment, a tall, red double-decker bus was careening at warp speed right towards Westgate's arch. We found ourselves holding our breath, as if that would help the driver. Then our mouths gaped open as the bus flew through, with just enough clearance to emerge on the other side unscathed. If the windows had been open, the passengers inside could've probably stuck out their hands and touched the stone as they flew through.

"Oh my God!" Kathy and I screamed.

"How's that for some English driving?! It always gives the American students heart failure," Colin shouted.

Now that we were safely on the other side of Westgate, we saw that the terraced houses had become small shops and restaurants. Two Indian ones, The Momtaz and The Curry Garden, were literally side by side.

"How on earth can two Indian restaurants survive like that, right next to each other?" I said to Colin.

"Oh, we English love a good curry. They both do a roaring trade, I can assure you. You'll see – they're absolutely heaving after time is called at the pubs. They stay open until 1am or later. Has either of you ever had an Indian meal? No? Well, that's going straight to the top of your list of things to do."

For now, though, the night's outing to the pub was enough. I could tell that after a few drinks, the jet lag was going to hit hard and I'd want to do nothing else but crawl into bed. "Here we are," Colin announced, as we arrived at The Falstaff Tap. The building itself was not the quaint, picturesque one I'd imagined, but the wooden sign hanging from an iron bracket over the door was promising: it was a portrait of a large, jolly, florid-faced man who was hoisting a full pint glass and in the midst of a belly laugh. My first English pub! I couldn't wait to get inside.

What a disappointment.

I'd built up and romanced the English pub experience to such an extent in my imagination that what faced me now was a complete bummer. The room I was standing in was completely devoid of any semblance of Olde England. The wooden floors were stained, scratched, and dull. The tables and chairs looked more like old packing crates than actual pieces of furniture. There wasn't a single overstuffed sofa or upholstered chair in the place. And where was the fireplace with the roaring fire? The brass railings and trimmings on the bar were in desperate need of a good polish. Framed photos of modern-day celebrities decorated the walls; no antique maps or prints of hunting scenes here. Other than a dart board, The Falstaff Tap was, in a single word, charmless. If this was the typical studenty pub, I wasn't impressed.

Colin quickly said, "I didn't want to take you too far out because I know that you and Kathy are tired. I promise that we're going to go for a traditional Sunday pub lunch at one of the most authentic country pubs you'll ever see. It will more than make up for the cheap and cheerful version tonight. Will that do?"

"Oh Colin, cheap and cheerful is perfect for tonight, and I can't wait to have a Sunday pub lunch. You've been so great today." I was embarrassed – my new friend was being nothing short of the perfect gentleman, and here I was looking like an ingrate.

"Not a word more about it," Colin replied. "Now, what would you girls like to drink? First round's on me."

Buying Rounds

This English custom quickly grew on us American students over the coming months. It makes so much more sense than everybody paying for their own drinks or trying to split a bar tab evenly at the end of a night.

Everyone in your group takes a turn going up to the bar and buying everyone else in the group a drink. Over the course of an evening, each person ends up spending more or less the same amount of money.

"Well, I'm definitely not a beer person," I replied. "What was that cider stuff you mentioned before?"

"Cider is a perfect drink for your first trip to an English pub. You can get sweet or dry. Which would you like to try?"

"What do you recommend?"

"Well, I quite like the dry. The sweet is a little over the top for my taste."

"Dry it is, then. Kathy and I will go find seats, O.K.?"

We found some spots over near a window and watched a group of students play darts. "I hear that most of the pubs have a dartboard," I said to Kathy. "I don't know about you, but there's a reason I went out for the high school track team instead of a sport that requires hand-eye coordination. I think I might be really dangerous if I tried to throw those things."

Kathy laughed. "I was just thinking the same thing. Nobody

in this place would be safe."

Colin arrived with our drinks on a small tray. "So what are you girls laughing about?"

"Kathy and I were just saying that jet lag, drinking, and sharp flying objects might be a very bad combination for us and you tonight," I answered, motioning to the dart game going on across the room.

"Too right! Those lads over there are pretty serious – they play in the university's dart club. But just you wait. By next June you'll be experts. Just make sure you have someone other than me teach you. I'm awful."

I looked at the tray with our drinks; something was definitely amiss here. Colin's glass was very tall and wide, but Kathy and I had glasses about half the size of his. "Hey, what's with the kid-sized glasses for us?" I joked. "We're thirsty."

"I'm only looking out for you both. You'll thank me tomorrow morning. Trust me. Our cider is quite strong – especially when you've been used to drinking that non-alcoholic stuff that you Yanks call cider. And I'm a bit old-fashioned, I admit. These half-pints are more, er…."

"Oh, I get it!" I realized where Colin was going with this. "So nice girls don't drink pints, is that it?"

Colin turned beet-red, much to our amusement. "Well, my mum's generation would certainly say so."

"We're only teasing you, Colin," I said. "I think that's sweet. So on my first date with an English guy, I'll make sure I stick with the half-pints. American girls have kind of a reputation over here, right?"

Colin squirmed with embarrassment. "Now, I never said

that. But – how shall I put this without causing offense? No one ever accused the Yanks of being shy. You're not backwards in coming forwards, if you see what I mean."

"Oooh, I like that much better than just coming out and calling names. The English are so much more subtle." I would have to start writing these things down. "O.K. so tell us what you're drinking, Mr. Full Pint, so that when Kathy and I buy the next rounds we'll sound like we know what we're talking about."

"Right. My drink is a lager top. It's lager beer that's been topped off with a little bit of lemonade."

"Lemonade? That sounds disgusting."

"No, it's not lemonade like you know it. Ours is fizzy – more like what you call Sprite at home."

"Oh, O.K. – sort of like a beer spritzer?"

"No, that's what we'd call a lager shandy – half lager, half lemonade. It's actually quite refreshing in the summer. That's what a lot of ladies will drink."

"In half-pint glasses, of course," I said mischievously.

"Naturally. Unless you're an American." Colin replied with a smirk.

"Oh, *touché*. So is lager the only kind of beer you can get in the pubs?"

"No, there's something called bitter, too. See that drink over there?" Colin pointed to the table next to us. A student was drinking from a full pint glass containing an amber-colored liquid. "See how it's almost orange compared to the yellow lager I'm drinking? And then there's stout – Guinness."

"Oh, yeah – my dad likes to have that sometimes."

I looked around the pub and noticed a distinct absence of wine glasses and mixed drinks. Everybody seemed to be on beer or cider. "So is wine not a big hit in England? And what about mixed drinks? I don't see any of those, either."

"Oh, wine and spirits are a bit dear for the student wallet. But yes, you can order them in the pubs – although you'll find a wider selection of them in the wine bars."

Say what?
Brit/Yank Translator

Dear: *expensive*

"So they don't serve beer and cider in the wine bars?"

"They serve everything. It's just that the wine bars are a little more posh. There's a wine bar called Tascoll's here in Canterbury. We can go there when the Beaujolais arrives."

"When who arrives?"

"Not who. What. Beaujolais is a really lovely, red French wine. The new vintage comes out every autumn, and all the pubs, wine bars, and off-licenses try to get it in before everyone else does. Some people in England even fly down to France just so they can be the first to bring the new Beaujolais back. It turns into quite a competition."

"Wow! All that for a bottle of wine? Let's see... lager, bitter, Guinness, wine, and mixed drinks. Anything else?"

"Hmmmmmmm. Let me think. Oh yes – I forgot the snake bite and snake bite black."

At this, Kathy piped up, "They sound a little dangerous."

"They are," Colin replied. "Snake bites are half a pint of lager and half a pint of cider in one pint glass. Very potent indeed. A snake bite black is the same with a little bit of blackcurrant juice added on the top."

"A pint glass," Kathy observed. "So it's not a girl drink."

"No - I can safely say that I've never personally seen a lady drink either of those."

Now it was Colin's turn to ask questions. He asked Kathy and me if we had met before we arrived in England, since our home colleges were nearby each other.

"No – we only met this afternoon," Kathy answered. "UMass is really big – it's bigger than some cities."

"Did a lot of you come over from UMass this year?"

"Yes, there are maybe a couple of dozen of us here. I know a few of them, but I'm not really friends with them. The rest of my friends stayed back in America. I was the only one who wanted to study abroad."

"Me too!" I said.

"So do you girls have some travel plans for this year?"

"Well, I'm not sure about Kathy, but I want to see as much as I can in the coming year. It's so great that you can take a ferry or plane and be in another country in no time. Kind of like us hopping in the car and driving to Vermont or New Hampshire, I guess. Only way more exciting."

"It would be cool to see Italy," Kathy mused.

"That's on my list, too. And I think Portugal and Morocco would be really different."

"What about right here in England?" Colin said. "Anything in mind?"

"London, definitely," I said right away. "I got to see it for a quick visit back in 1982, when I visited my pen pal. But the IRA had just bombed Hyde Park, so my pen pal's mom was a little nervous about spending a lot of time there. My *Let's Go* book says that Canterbury is really close to London by train. So that'll be fun for day trips."

"The Canterbury East and Canterbury West rail stations will both get you there in about an hour or so, depending on whether you get a fast or slow train," Colin said.

"Oh good! I'm really excited to see London."

"I'm psyched to see Hadrian's Wall and Scotland," Kathy added. "And Ireland, too."

"Oh, I'd like to do that, too" I said. "You know, Kathy, we have a really long break at Christmas. Maybe we could go backpacking together. I'm not going back home for the holidays. Are you?"

"No – I'm staying here in England. That would be cool to have somebody to travel with."

"So Diane, I gather from your surname of Giombetti that you're of Italian descent. Have you any relatives in Italy?"

"Yeah – some of my grandfather's cousins on my dad's side are still over there, just outside Milan. One of my dad's brothers met them when he was backpacking through Europe, but that was a long time ago – I was really little."

"And Kathy, what about you?" Colin asked. "Where does your family originally come from?"

"Finland. I don't think anybody keeps in touch with our relatives over there – that's assuming there are any left."

"Have you ever been there?"

"No, Colin – have you?"

"Sadly, I've never been anywhere in Scandinavia. Never mind – there's plenty of time to see the world after I get my degree."

"Are you going to do an around-the-world backpacking trip after you graduate?" I asked. Allison had told me that a lot of British students took off for a year to see the world before returning to England to get real jobs. It sounded exciting.

"I'd quite like to do that, but I haven't decided yet. I may get the real job first and then save up some money so I can afford to stay in hotels once in a while and not hostels all the time."

"So what kind of a job do you think you want after you graduate? Will you use your American Studies degree?" I asked.

"I think insurance is interesting, or maybe banking – I won't make any big decisions until early spring, though, when all of the big companies come to campus to set up interviews."

"They do that at Mount Holyoke, too," I said. "I have no

54

idea what I'm going to do. I'm not sure about grad school. I don't think the world needs another Shakespearean scholar. Maybe I'll go into advertising – I'd be using my English major, but it seems like all the big agencies are in New York City. I can't see myself living there."

"What about you, Kathy?" Colin wondered. "What do you study at home? Have you any plans for life after UMass?"

"I'm in the physics program, so I'll probably go on to grad school and then do post-grad research."

"Well, we're a pretty well-rounded lot, I think. Here's to a fun year." Colin raised his glass and we joined him. "Cheers!"

Two rounds later, Kathy and I were starting to nod off. The jet lag and the cider were catching up with us. I was glad now that Colin had been old-fashioned and chivalrous. A pint and a half of British cider was more than enough for me – I couldn't imagine what I'd feel like if I'd had three pints.

"What do you say we get you two back to your rooms?" Colin suggested. "Aren't there some entertainments that the university's laid on for the Americans tomorrow?"

"Yes – we're going on a tour of Canterbury Cathedral after lunch, I think, with some time in the city afterwards. The day after that, they're taking us to Leeds Castle."

"Well, it certainly would be bad form to show up in the cathedral with a hangover, so perhaps we should leave now."

I truly don't remember a whole lot about the walk back up the hill to the university – except that it seemed much longer than the way down. Colin offered to hail a cab, but Kathy and I said no. Unnecessary expenses like that would quickly eat away at our savings.

We dropped Kathy off at her room first, and then Colin walked me back to mine. "Thanks for an awesome day, Colin," I said through an enormous yawn. "Allison was right – I am in good hands."

"My pleasure. I imagine you'll want a lie-in tomorrow, so why don't I come knock you up at lunchtime, then?"

Say what?
Brit/Yank Translator

Lie-in:
to sleep late
Knock someone up:
to knock on their door

I was jolted out of my stupor. Surely he hadn't just said what I thought I'd heard? "You most certainly will not!" I yelped. "O.K., I'm sure that what you just said is something perfectly innocent over here. But if we were back home, you would've just announced that you planned to, um, get me pregnant at lunchtime tomorrow."

"Oh God, I've really put my foot in it," Colin gasped. "Those were most definitely not my intentions."

"It's O.K., Colin." I'd started laughing. "This is one for my journal. I can see it now: '...*new friend offers to father my child on the first night we've met.*' And here I was thinking you British were so reserved and stuffy. On second thought, why don't you just go back to 'collecting' me? I think I prefer that to getting knocked up."

"Right you are. Sleep well, Diane, and see you tomorrow."

Back in my room, I weighed going straight to bed against trudging back down the hall to the bathroom to wash my face and brush my teeth. It was so tempting to call it a night right now. But I knew how disgusting I'd feel the next morning. Grabbing my bathroom stuff, I headed down the hall to do battle with the hot and cold taps. With some luck, I'd emerge without third-degree burns on my face.

Know Before You Go

A Journal: Don't Leave Home Without One

Even if you're not much of a writer, be sure to take a journal with you on your junior year abroad. It can be as fancy as a beautifully bound leather volume or as simple as an empty, spiral-bound notebook. Every time you go somewhere, meet a new person, or have a fun adventure, jot down a few lines about the experience so you won't forget about it. If the spirit moves you, write more than a few lines.

If your journal has a built-in memorabilia pocket or two (and many of them do these days), fill it with items such as ticket stubs, menus, and printed cocktail napkins – anything that helps you remember the sights, sounds, and smells of what you were doing at the time.

Years later, when your junior year abroad days are long behind you, that journal and memorabilia will become a priceless time capsule of an incredible year in your life. Combine them with your photos and you'll have the makings of an amazing scrapbook.

✧ Chapter Five ✧

I woke with a start the next morning and reached for the little alarm clock I'd brought from home. My parents had wanted to buy me a real travel clock for my junior year abroad, but I'd insisted on packing the little wind-up alarm clock with the brass bells on the top that I'd had since my seventh birthday. It was lavender, one of my favorite colors, with little hands that glowed green in the dark. Of course, I'd forgotten to put the clock five hours ahead before I fell into bed last night – so I lay there staring dumbly at it for a minute or two until I remembered that the hands still showed the time back at home.

I re-set them. Over here, it was now...time to get into the shower! I got up and grabbed the slip of paper on my desk that showed the dining hall's serving hours. Lunch would be starting soon. If I was quick, I could be cleaned up and ready before Colin arrived. Nothing like feeling as if you'd been shot out of a cannon. I'd slept right through breakfast! But Colin had been right. I didn't have that dopey, jet lag feeling anymore.

Today was going to be a great day – there was the trip to the cathedral and around Canterbury, and then after dinner we'd be going to another pub with Arvine and her friends. This being 1986, I thought to myself, *I need to buy some extra rolls of film*, as I walked down the hall into the bathroom and put my things in the shower room. There was a full roll in my camera and two additional rolls I'd brought from home, but I'd probably go through them quickly.

I pulled back the shower curtain to turn on the faucet and stopped cold. In a big mess on the floor where the drain should've been was a huge clump of dark, spiral curls of hair.

"Gross!" I yelled out loud. I kicked it aside. Who wanted to look at that nasty mess? I'd have to let the floor's student adviser hear about that.

When Colin arrived to collect me for lunch, I asked him, "So how do you know who your floor's student adviser is? I didn't see any signs on anyone's door." There was a blank stare from Colin.

"We don't have those," he replied.

"Well, what about dorm meetings with the hall president? You must have them? You know, everyone who lives in Keynes gets together once a month and you talk about things like cleaning up after your messes and remembering quiet hours." At Mount Holyoke, we had student advisers on each floor – they did things like mediate in minor roommate disputes and ensure that the floor's common areas stayed clean. Our hall presidents were also students. But they had bigger-picture responsibilities, like encouraging overall dorm safety.

My question was met with another blank look from Colin, and then he started laughing his head off. "Oh dear, Diane – you are going to have quite an education over here, and I don't mean in the classroom. I'm not taking the mick, really. But you Americans are funny with your student advisers and hall presidents. If you have a problem with somebody on your corridor here, you have to fix it yourself. Has something awful happened?"

Suddenly, my "problem" seemed a little silly. "Sorry, Colin. God, I'm sounding high-maintenance, aren't I? I think I can take care of this one myself." I ripped a piece of paper out of a

Say what?
Brit/Yank Translator

Taking the mick
(also taking the mickey):
to make fun of someone

notebook that was on my bookshelf, and scrawled on it, *PLEASE CLEAN UP YOUR HAIR – THE REST OF US HAVE TO USE THIS SHOWER AFTER YOU!!!* Then I took a thumbtack off my bulletin board. "Wait here," I told Colin. "I'll be right back." I marched down the hall, into the bathroom, and tacked my note on the outside of the shower room door. There – problem solved. In a non-confrontational, passive-aggressive way, anyhow. "Come on, I'm starving," I said to a baffled Colin when I returned. "Let's go eat."

After lunch, all of the American students gathered outside in front of Keynes College, where several coaches were waiting to take us into Canterbury. We felt a little like VIPs. A group of official-looking people stood at a distance from the students. One of the men in the group stepped forward and briefly addressed all of us before we piled into the coaches.

"Good afternoon, everyone – I'm Rod Smithson, the director of the university's international students program. On behalf of my colleagues, I'd like to welcome you to the University of Kent at Canterbury. I trust you've all had an opportunity to unpack and make yourselves at home? We're thrilled to have you for the coming year and we want to help you make the most of your exchange program.

"Before the real orientation activities begin, we thought you'd enjoy a tour of Canterbury's magnificent cathedral. The dean has kindly arranged for us to have a private tour of not only the cathedral, but the Chapter House, as well." He paused here, and waited for us to act suitably impressed. "After that, we'll take a short walking tour of the city so you can get your bearings. Shall we start?" He turned and sprang onto the first coach, followed by his posse.

Kathy, Julie, and I climbed into a coach, followed by an American guy named Bob, who lived on Kathy's corridor, but on the other side of the fire doors. Julie had met Bob at breakfast this morning, while Kathy and I were sleeping off our ciders. "Bob's from Indiana University," Julie said. "Kathy said your British friend Colin studied there last year."

"Hi, Bob. Yes, Colin did do a year at IU – he said he had a great year there. I think he really misses America. Are there a lot of you here from IU?"

"About six or seven of us," Bob answered. He was tall and athletic-looking, with broad shoulders and a movie-star smile. "So you're from Massachusetts, same as Kathy?"

"That's right. Different college, though – Mount Holyoke."

"Oh. Isn't that a fancy girls' school?"

Bob and I were not getting off to a good start. "It's not a girls' school. It's a women's college – the oldest one in the U.S.," I corrected him. I sighed and rolled my eyes at Kathy, who rolled her eyes back in sympathy.

"Sorry. No offense."

The coaches made their way down the hill and approached Westgate. Kathy and I decided that being inside a coach as it flew through the arch was almost as hair-raising as watching one scream through from the sidewalk. I found myself shutting my eyes until we came out safely on the other side.

The coaches were now inching slowly down the High Street, and a quick look out my window revealed why: there seemed to be more pedestrians on the street than cars. In fact, there were so many people on foot that there wasn't enough room on the sidewalks for everybody; the overflow simply spilled right out onto the High Street, with people getting out of the way of cars whenever things got a little too close for comfort.

"Wow, I don't think I've ever seen anything like this," I said to Kathy. "Look at all these people." We were sitting at the front of the bus and the driver overheard me.

"Oh, this is nothing, love," he said. "Just you wait 'til the coachloads of French schoolchildren invade on their day trips. That'll be starting soon. Swarms of 'em, I tell you. They take the ferries from Calais to Dover, pile into their coaches, and make straight for Canterbury. Every one of the blighters as rude and smelly as the next. Sod the lot of 'em."

"I see that English-French relations haven't improved since the Hundred Years War," I whispered to Kathy.

We came to a stop a short while later, and the driver announced, "Here we are, ladies and gents." Everyone got to their feet and began to make their way down the aisle and off the bus.

"I don't see the cathedral," one girl remarked to her seatmate. "Isn't that where we're supposed to be going? This is just a street. Where are they taking us?"

"If you would all kindly assemble over here, please – that's right, thank you. We don't want to lose any of you on your first day in Canterbury!" Rod Smithson announced over the chatter. "We're just going to wait 'til the coaches drive off. There, that's better. Lovely!" He swept his arms up in a grand gesture, as if he were getting ready to hug all of us at once. Something big was about to happen, evidently.

"We are standing at the corner of High Street and Mercery Lane," he continued. "This is one of the most dramatic approaches to the cathedral. I dare say that by year's end, all of you will have this very shot in your scrapbooks and photo albums." He pointed down what we assumed was Mercery Lane: an absolutely tiny, narrow medieval street that looked more like an alley than anything else.

"If you'll please follow me, you'll soon see exactly what I mean." Rod took off down Mercery Lane with the rest of us in tow. This was an amazing little street. It was hard to keep from tripping and bumping into other people, because I wanted to look up, straight ahead, and next to me all at the same time. There was so much to see.

Mercery Lane seemed to defy the laws of physics. The upper jetties of the medieval buildings on each side of the lane looked as if they were built by a three-year-old who was in a big hurry to move on to his next project with his blocks. The buildings leaned into each other. In fact, the overhanging stories of the buildings on the opposing sides of the lane were nearly touching. On the ground floors were all kinds of retail shops that we'd later come to know and love: Boots the Chemist, Sock Shop, and Colorbox.

Many of these shops had bay or bow windows with the old-fashioned dimples in their square glass panes. We got a tantalizing glance at the displays in each storefront. Shoppers clutching bags ducked in and out, making the scene that much more interesting and chaotic.

Of course, since the sidewalks on Mercery Lane were almost as narrow as the lane itself, we all followed Rod's lead and just walked down the middle of the street. I thought to myself that you'd have to be crazy to even attempt driving a car down this alley.

Suddenly, one of the Americans said, "Ooooooh, look up ahead! You can just see the top of the cathedral!" We'd all been so distracted by Mercery Lane that we'd completely forgotten our final destination. As we got farther down the lane and the foot traffic started to thin out, we began to catch small glimpses of the top of the cathedral's magnificent bell tower and its gorgeous lacy spires. You could feel everybody's excitement and suspense.

At the end of the lane, we spilled out into a large, open square complete with a statue and a fountain. Curving off to our right and left at the edges of the square were even more shops. I saw a couple of pub signs and some restaurants, as well. And facing us, across the square, was what could only be described as the biggest, grandest front door I'd ever seen. It was the focal point of the square, and appeared to be carved out of stone that had weathered a soft grey.

"We are now standing in the Buttermarket Square. You're looking at Christchurch Gate, which was built in 1517. It's the monumental entrance to the cathedral precincts," Rod shouted, as he ushered us across the busy square to the statue and fountain.

Yes, monumental is exactly the right word for this, I thought. At eye level, there was beautiful carving and delicate windows. Higher up was a band of brightly painted crests or shields, each with its own design and color scheme. Above that was more carving and some additional windows. Higher still, a second band featured a parade of carved angels in various poses, all with differently colored robes. Two tall towers rose out of the very top of Christchurch Gate.

Christchurch Gate as it looked when I saw it in 2012.
Note the new Christ in majesty statue, added (to my dismay)
when the gate was restored in 1991.

"You know, it looks just like the front of a castle, except the rest of the castle is missing," somebody behind me commented. "These carvings and shields that you see are dedicated to Prince Arthur, who was the older brother of one Prince Henry," Rod noted. "When Prince Arthur died in 1502, Henry succeeded to the throne and assumed a much more famous title: King Henry the Eighth."

Something was out of place with Christchurch Gate, though. In the middle of the band with all of the carved angels, there was a gaping, empty nook that had once obviously contained a huge statue. It looked strange to see a bare space in the middle of something that was otherwise so ornately decorated.

"That hole you see up there housed a figure of Christ in majesty," explained Rod. "Sadly, the statue was destroyed in 1642 by Parliamentarians. We're going to proceed through Christchurch Gate and into the cathedral precincts. Come this way, everybody." He led us under and through a high arch that was carved into the gate.

"Why don't they just replace the old statue?" a girl near me asked the one walking beside her.

"Oh sure – the cathedral people will just drive down to Medieval Statues R Us and pick one up," cracked some wiseass.

"Jerk," the girl said. "It was just a question."

"A stupid one," Kathy said softly to me. "There are these things called conservation and restoration...hello! There should be a law that Americans like her can't study abroad. It makes the rest of us look bad."

Now that we were in the precincts, we had an up-close and unobstructed view of the cathedral from its western entrance.

It was breathtaking. All we could do was just stand there staring with our mouths hanging open. I couldn't wait to take my parents here when they came out the following spring. I held up my camera and took the first of the many photos I'd snap of the cathedral.

Many years and many trips back to the cathedral later, that first shot I took on that October afternoon back in 1986 is still my favorite. The sky was cobalt blue and nearly cloudless, making the beigey-white stone of the cathedral leap out in sharp contrast.

The other thing I noticed as we neared the cathedral's entrance was how green and perfectly clipped the surrounding lawns were. They were cut so close that the blades of grass barely rose above the ground. What's more, there wasn't a single weed, dandelion, or patch of crabgrass anywhere in sight. It was perfect.

At that moment, all I could think of was what my dad would say when he saw this scene. Back at home, our "lawn" (and I use that term loosely) was the source of much laughter between me and my sisters and much embarrassment to our poor mom. When my parents built their home and we all moved in, my dad somehow never got around to rototilling, seeding, and cultivating a real front or back lawn.

Instead, crabgrass, other weeds, and moss slowly appeared, took over, and then gradually filled in at the front and back until there was a green, uniform ground cover. If you looked at it from a distance, it really did resemble a lawn. Whenever it started getting a little unruly, Dad would grab the lawnmower and make things look more presentable.

"What are you laughing at?" Kathy asked.

"Oh, nothing. Just a family joke," I said.

As we entered the cathedral and stared down its cavernous nave, I was immediately struck by its overwhelming vastness: we were, quite literally, swallowed up by it. Looking up, all I could see were great, rising columns that flared into a web of soaring fan vaults in the ceiling high above me. I actually felt dizzy and had to look down for a moment so I could see and feel the hard flagstone under my feet.

Far ahead of us was a shallow set of stairs and a wide altar with a pulpit off to the side. The effect made the area seem like the stage of a theatre waiting for a performance to begin.

The other thing I noticed as we waited for our tour to get underway was that the space we were now standing in was completely bathed in light. It poured down on us in long, golden shafts through the magnificent, medieval stained-glass windows. The light was so bright that I could see individual dust motes spilling along the shafts.

Then there was the sound, or the lack of it. Rod told us that the cathedral was surrounded by its own close, a collection of houses, offices, and outbuildings where the cathedral's deans, vergers, and other key staff live and work. There was a lot of traffic in the close, and, as you might imagine, a huge number of people and their cars coming and going at all hours of the day. The minute that we entered the cathedral and the door shut tight behind us, however, all of that outside noise was muffled by the thickness of the cathedral's stone walls. It was as if everything had stopped on the outside.

Inside there was a reverent hush and a calm stillness that made me feel very small and very safe at the same time. This was a place where kings, queens, and princes had been honored, where an archbishop was martyred, and where generations of pilgrims came after treacherous journeys to pay homage at his shrine. The very floors we were standing on were weathered tombstones of the dead who had lain buried underneath for hundreds of years. Our voices automatically dropped to whispers.

I walked over to one of the enormous columns nearby and reached out my hand: the column was cool to the touch and mirror-smooth. It completely blew me away to think that this gorgeous, massive building had been constructed nearly 1,000 years ago entirely by hand, without modern aids like power tools or hydraulic cranes. I'd been prepared to be impressed by the cathedral, but I hadn't expected to be so moved.

Our private tour was fascinating. Although I'd read some of Chaucer's *Canterbury Tales*, I didn't realize just how important this site was to England's Christian history. In 597, our guide told us, St. Augustine arrived on Kent's shores to introduce Christianity to Britain. He'd been sent from Rome by Pope Gregory the Great, and made his way to Canterbury, which he'd chosen for the seat of his mission. The word "cathedral" actually comes from the Latin word *cathedra*, which means "seat".

Augustine eventually had a cathedral built and became the very first Archbishop of Canterbury. Over the next several centuries, Saxons rebuilt and enlarged Augustine's original building. A fire in the early 11th century destroyed Augustine's cathedral, and the Normans, under the leadership of Archbishop Lanfranc, had completely rebuilt the cathedral by 1077. You can still see parts of the Norman structure today.

We learned that although Canterbury had long been part of the original pilgrims' route to Rome, it was catapulted to fame and became a destination in its own right by the martyrdom of Archbishop Thomas Becket, who lived during the reign of a much earlier King Henry – Henry II. Becket had been appointed Archbishop by his old friend Henry, and this, our guide explained, is when things began to go downhill for Becket.

The Archbishop found that serving two masters – the Pope and King Henry II – was not easy. He was caught between his loyalties to the Pope and Rome on one side, and to the King on the other. The Pope and Rome won, of course, much to the King's rage. The relationship between Becket and Henry II grew increasingly strained and reached a breaking point late in 1170. Henry, in one of his famous tempers, reportedly screamed the ill-fated words, "Who will rid me of this meddlesome priest?!"

Four of Henry's knights overheard his rant and set out to grant their king's wish. They immediately left France, where the King and his court were spending Christmas, sailed for England, and rode at great speed to Canterbury. On the terrible night of December 29th, 1170, the knights entered the cathedral, where the Archbishop was kneeling in prayer. They struck him in the head three times with their swords. According to a monk's eyewitness testimony, the third blow broke off the tip of one of the knights' sword.

Legend has it that as Becket fell, his head hit the floor of the cathedral with such force that it cracked the stone on impact. Seeing that the Archbishop was dead, the knights fled the scene.

About three days after the Archbishop's grisly murder, a series of miracles started being attributed to him. It wasn't long before a shrine had been erected in Becket's honor, and pilgrims began arriving to pray, pay tribute, and seek its reputed healing powers. Much to King Henry's horror, Becket's power and fame increased tenfold in death. By 1173, the martyred Archbishop had been canonized by the Pope, and thousands upon thousands of devoted pilgrims were pouring into Canterbury.

Our guide led us to the site of Becket's murder. This area, now called The Martyrdom, was dignified in its stark simplicity, considering the amazing repercussions of what had happened there. A small altar, nothing more than a kneeler, really, had been installed in the corner where the killing took place. An eternity candle burned on it, and a plain commemorative plaque had been fixed to the wall above. A conspicuous section of the stone floor nearby was, indeed, cracked.

"King Henry II must have felt partly to blame for Becket's murder, right?" somebody quietly asked the guide. "I mean, he didn't come right out and kill the Archbishop himself, but the murder wouldn't have happened if the King hadn't been heard flipping out about Becket."

"Interestingly put, young man," the guide observed wryly. "And true. Henry had a real crisis on his hands. His subjects were flocking to Becket's shrine. Rome was furious; the Pope was seriously considering excommunication for Henry II. Public opinion was not in the King's favor. Henry realized he had to show remorse if he wanted to keep hold of the throne and avoid the Pope's wrath. So he made a personal pilgrimage of his own to Canterbury to demonstrate his remorse publicly.

"He arrived on horseback at the Westgate, dressed in sackcloth like a humble pilgrim. Then he got down from his horse and walked barefoot to the cathedral, where he prostrated himself at Becket's shrine, begged for forgiveness, and allowed himself to be flogged. It was a dramatic, brilliantly calculated spectacle. And it worked – it saved his reign."

Becket was big business; his shrine became one of the richest in Europe and was said to be encrusted with gold and jewels. By the 1530s, its wealth and value had caught the eye of greedy King Henry VIII, who eagerly plundered its treasures when he ordered its dissolution in 1538.

"Nobody knows exactly what happened to all of those valuables," our tour guide concluded, "except that they ended up in the King's treasury, of course." A famously huge cut ruby that had adorned the shrine reportedly ended up being set into a ring for one of Henry VIII's fat fingers.

But that was just the beginning of our cathedral tour. From the Martyrdom, our guide led us around to various royal tombs, including the one of Edward, the Black Prince – his helmet, gloves, and chain mail were even displayed above his sarcophagus. We visited several chapels, including a beautiful one whose vaulted ceiling was decorated to resemble a night sky dotted with tiny gold stars.

The cathedral's medieval stained-glass windows were our next stop. They were another of its major attractions, and although many of them were destroyed or badly damaged over the centuries, enough had survived or been carefully restored that they were still arresting in their beauty. I couldn't get over how brilliant the colors were and I marveled at the workmanship it took to produce these masterpieces. I could've spent the entire afternoon staring at them, but our guide had other plans for us.

"We're now descending into the cathedral crypt, which contains, among other things, the cathedral's treasury – all of the gold, silver, and plate as well as antiquarian books and other priceless documents and artifacts," he noted. "For some visitors, the crypt is their favorite part of the cathedral. Occasionally, evensong takes place down here."

"What's evensong?" I asked. I'd never heard of that before, and figured it must be something that was specific to the Church of England.

"Oh, it's a most lovely choral tradition that takes place in the cathedrals and churches across Great Britain in the late afternoon or early evenings during the week," he replied. "Do try to attend while you're here in Canterbury this year. You'll hear hymns and Bible lessons put to music. There are readings from Scripture, as well. It's a wonderful way to pass an hour.

"And you must attend the university's Christmas caroling service," he continued. "It's held right here in the cathedral, in the main part where you first came in. It takes place entirely by candlelight and happens right before the Christmas break."

I couldn't even imagine how beautiful the cathedral must look by candlelight. The Christmas caroling service and evensong both got added to my mental "to do" list, which was growing by the minute.

Before we left the crypt, I took another long look around. The feeling down here was the opposite of the space in the cathedral "upstairs." Whereas the main cathedral was full of soaring columns, graceful Gothic arches and high ceilings, the crypt had low ceilings, very little in the way of decoration, and squat, chunky Romanesque arches. It was gloomy and mysterious down here; I could easily imagine a ghost or two prowling around at night. In fact, the only well-lit part of the crypt was the treasury. Bright track lights shone down on the rows and rows of shelves displaying their valuables, which were safely locked away behind glass walls that went from the floor to the ceiling.

"I don't know about you two, but the crypt kind of gives me the creeps," Kathy said to Julie and me. "I don't think I'd want to be down here by myself for too long."

"Me neither," echoed Julie.

Our group had already begun heading for the stairs that would take us back up to the cathedral when our guide announced, "I have one last treat for you. Before you leave, I'm going to show you round the cloisters and then take you briefly to the Chapter House. These aren't usually parts of the tour."

"Oh wow! I didn't think we'd get to see those," I said to Kathy and Julie. "Did you see the pictures in the viewbook where all the third-years are standing in the cloisters in their caps and gowns? They graduate right here in the cathedral. How cool is that?"

"It sure beats the football stadium at UMass," Kathy replied.

By the end of our exhaustive tour, we'd spent such a long time indoors that we found ourselves squinting against the afternoon sun as we emerged from the Chapter House. Rod Smithson and his crew were waiting for us so that we could take a short walking tour of the other interesting sites in Canterbury.

"Well, did you enjoy your visit to the cathedral?" he asked, and began laughing when all of us starting answering him at once. I think that for many of us, the sheer age of the cathedral was the most amazing thing about it. It was starting to sink in that "old" in the United States and "old" in England were entirely different things.

"Yes, we do have rather a lot of history here," Rod agreed. "And you haven't even seen Canterbury's Roman ruins. England was one of the outposts of the Roman Empire – there were fortresses and villas all over the countryside, and lots of those famously straight Roman roads, as well. You can't have a roadworks or building project in Canterbury without unearthing some ancient artifact. Before the city undertakes any major building project, the archaeologists get to come in and set up a dig. It's quite fascinating to watch. I should imagine you'll get to see them at work quite a lot in the coming months."

Again, I was embarrassed by my own ignorance; when I thought of England's vast history, the first things that came to my mind were Chaucer, Shakespeare, knights, castles, and, more recently, The Blitz and The Battle of Britain. I'd never even considered that the Romans had been here way before all of that. I had a lot to learn.

"Before we return to the coaches," continued Rod, "we thought a short walking tour of Canterbury might be fun. We'll be covering a lot, but the wonderful thing is you have the rest of the academic year to explore it all. Let's start, shall we?"

We could easily spend our entire year abroad just exploring England, if Canterbury was any indication. Our "short" walking tour took us to the remaining sections of the city's original walls and the beautiful Dane John park and gardens below the ramparts. We caught a brief glimpse of Canterbury Castle, an old ruin that seemed to be undergoing conservation or restoration of some kind (though I didn't see any archeologists busily working away with their tiny picks and brushes). We also saw the Queen Elizabeth I Tea Room, a medieval house with a plaque informing passersby that the monarch had eaten and stayed there briefly in 1573 (kind of like the "George Washington slept here" plaques that are on lots of old buildings at home).

I especially liked the Weavers Houses, half-timbered buildings that leaned at crazy angles over the River Stour, which flowed lazily through the center of the city. Rod told us that the houses were once inhabited by Huguenots, Protestants from Flanders (now part of modern-day Belgium) who fled religious persecution and found sanctuary in England. They were skilled textile artisans who set up their looms in these buildings along the river and became wealthy merchants.

Someone in our group noticed that one of the Weavers Houses had a long pole sticking out of it that jutted out above the river. At the end of the pole was something that looked an awful lot like the top of an old, wooden high chair. When we asked Rod about it, he explained that it was a ducking stool.

"Ducking stools were a form of public humiliation and punishment," he said. "But they had a darker side, too. Sometimes they were used to prove if people were witches."

"How did they do that?" a student asked.

"Well it was far from scientific and offered no proof of guilt or innocence whatsoever. The accused was forced into the stool, and the pole was lowered, ducking the poor soul underwater for some time. If she survived the trial [the accused was almost always a woman] and was still alive when the pole was raised, it proved she was a witch. She was then promptly put to death. If the accused had drowned by the time the pole was raised, it proved she was innocent of the charges of witchcraft after all."

"But she was dead by then, so it wouldn't matter that she was innocent!" the same student protested. "She was toast either way. That's not fair."

"Of course it's not. Fairness had nothing to do with it."

"Whoa. Dude, that's harsh," observed a different student, whose sweatshirt, not surprisingly, was emblazoned with the words *University of Southern California*.

The last stop on our whirlwind walking tour was the Eastbridge Hospital of St. Thomas, where poorer pilgrims could find accommodation after their long journey to Canterbury.

"They were so poor they had to stay in a *hospital?*" asked a girl at the front.

"This wasn't a hospital in the modern-day sense of the word," Rod said patiently. "Back in the late 1100s, the word meant a place where you could find hospitality. You could sleep here for one night if you were healthy, but the accommodations were dormitory-style and were reserved especially for poor, crippled, homeless, or pregnant pilgrims."

The more well-off pilgrims, however, didn't have to worry about such basic conditions. They could afford to stay in one of Canterbury's many inns, taverns, or hotels. And while they were in the city, they had to eat and drink, of course, and would want to buy souvenirs of their pilgrimage. The city made a lot of money off the pilgrims. It was easy to understand how Becket's murder and his shrine had ended up making Canterbury so wealthy.

"But the guide at the cathedral told us that King Henry VIII confiscated all the riches from Becket's shrine and then destroyed it in the 1500s," another girl piped up. "So didn't that hurt all of the business owners who relied on the money that the pilgrims spent while they were in Canterbury?"

"Oh yes," said Rod. "The pilgrim industry dried up nearly overnight. Henry VIII desperately needed cash, and cathedrals like Canterbury, plus England's monasteries, were very wealthy. In 1538, the king ordered the dissolution of the monasteries — his men spread out all over the country and seized the treasures of all of the major religious centres."

Canterbury was especially rich, thanks to the huge income that all of the pilgrims provided when they came to visit Becket's shrine. Rod told us that according to records kept during the seizure, it took 26 wagons to carry off Canterbury's treasures alone. Henry VIII even forbade the publishing of Becket's name and image, as well as any further pilgrimages to the saint's shrine. The final blow to the city's pilgrim-based economy was when Henry ordered that Becket's bones should be burned.

"Eventually, other merchants and tradespeople set up business in Canterbury," Rod continued. "The Huguenot weavers were already here long before the suppression of the monasteries, for example. They were later joined by potters and leather tanners. There's still a tannery operating here today. You probably smelled it when we were walking along the city walls earlier on the tour."

By this time, most of us were exhausted from all of the walking we'd done; after all, it was still only our second full day in Canterbury. My head was spinning from all of the things we'd just seen and learned. I couldn't wait to make more trips back down into the city and explore everything on my own time. It was going to be really hard to concentrate on things as mundane as studying, once classes started up in a couple of days.

Canterbury's lovely Westgate Gardens, which we didn't visit much as students – probably because it was nowhere near a pub.

Another view of Canterbury's magnificent cathedral.
This shot includes the famous Bell Harry tower in the center.

Chapter Six

In the dining hall that evening, Julie, Kathy, Bob, and I kept Arvine and her friends entertained during dinner with stories about our cathedral and city tour. "Oh my, you lot certainly got the royal treatment," said Jeremy. "When we first arrived on campus three years ago, we had to tour the cathedral and city sights with all of the other English peasants. Being an international student certainly has its privileges. Luckily, those don't extend to the dining experience and all of this gourmet food."

"Don't listen to him," Hugh laughed. "He's just in a foul mood because his football team from home lost a big match today. He'll be back to his usual jolly self once we get a pint or two down him tonight."

Say what?
Brit/Yank Translator | **Football:** *soccer*

"So where's this pub we're going to?" I asked. "You said it's not studenty, like the Falstaff?"

"It's called The Dog and Bear," Arvine replied. "It's really lovely – we'll probably be the youngest people there, and almost certainly the only students."

"How did you find it?"

"We set out on a walk after dinner one evening during our first year, and there it was in the middle of a lane. We've been going pretty regularly ever since. I guess you could say that when we're here at uni, The Dog and Bear is our local."

"What's a local?" said Julie.

"You know, the pub where you and your friends always go. After a while, the landlord and the barmen get to know you. If you go often enough, sometimes they'll even hang your own private tankard on a hook from the ceiling above the bar for you."

"How neat! Do you have a tankard hanging there, Arvine?"

"No – I much prefer a snowball. It's a sort of mixed drink. We'll have to introduce you to one this evening."

I had no idea where The Dog and Bear was. Arvine had said it was a country pub, so it couldn't be anywhere in the city center. My guess was correct; to get there, we all walked down the long, main road of the university, but instead of turning left and heading down the hill towards Westgate, and the cathedral, we headed right and walked up.

"Are there hills all over Kent, or just here in Canterbury?" Kathy asked.

"I'm afraid that this is pretty typical of the countryside around here," Ben said. "In the spring, the Canterbury Half-Marathon goes through the city and the surrounding villages. They say it's one of the toughest courses in the country – on account of all of the hills."

"Great. I'll make sure not to sign up for that one."

I'm not sure how far we walked – maybe a mile or so. I do remember turning left shortly after the university's driveway. At some point we found ourselves in a residential area full of houses that Arvine called "bungalows." It seemed weird that there would be a pub in the middle of all this. At home the restaurants, night clubs, hotels, and bars were all packed together one right after another on major roads.

Say what?
Brit/Yank Translator

Bungalows:
ranch-style houses

"Here we are!" Arvine announced.

The Dog and Bear was suddenly right in front of us, along the lane we'd been walking down — just as Arvine had said. *Now this is more like it,* I thought as I looked around. What I was looking at was exactly what I'd imagined an English pub to be. It looked like a house, with the tile roofing and stucco exterior that would become so familiar to us. A string of fat, multicolored light bulbs, like the ones we used to have on our Christmas tree when I was a kid, glowed along the roofline and over the door.

The pub's sign, hanging above us near the front door, was adorable. It showed a bear standing up on its hind legs, with a dog at its feet. A chalkboard easel stood near the front door. Somebody had written "Live music. Real ale." on it. Things were looking promising.

When we walked in, we were immediately facing the bar. There was lots of comfortable-looking seating (upholstered chairs and stools! actual sofas!) throughout the entire pub. Off in a far corner, the musical act appeared to be setting up. I could just see through into another room, from where lots of laughter and shouts were coming— maybe there was a billiards table or some dartboards in there. The pub felt cozy, warm, welcoming, and old. I loved it right away.

"Hello! Lovely to have you back — how was your summer?" a voice called. It was the barman, or maybe the landlord, and he was waving at Arvine, Ben, Hugh, and Jeremy. He had a big smile on his face and his shirt sleeves were rolled up to his elbows. Everyone in the pub turned to look at us. It didn't seem like they got a whole lot of strangers around here, so I'm sure that Kathy, Julie, Bob, and I stuck out like sore thumbs.

Say what?
Brit/Yank Translator

Barman: *bartender*

"Summer was wonderful, John, thanks," answered Arvine. "We've brought some American friends with us tonight — they're studying with us at the university this year. We wanted to show them a proper country pub."

"And you picked this place? Ah, Crikey — you'll put your Yanks right off with the likes of these hooligans here!" The man behind the bar jerked his head at some older guys who were leaning against the bar and holding pint glasses. The men laughed loudly and went back to their drinking.

A stout, middle-aged woman with unruly gray hair and a dish towel tucked into the waist of her slacks walked up to all of us. "Well, who do we have here, then?" she said to Arvine. "'Bout time you lot showed up."

"Hello, Mandy!" said Arvine. "How've you been? I'd like you to meet Diane, Kathy, Julie, and Bob. They're exchange students from America."

86

"Pleasure to meet you all – when did you arrive?"

"Yesterday," Kathy answered. "And we're having a really good time so far."

"Well, I hope it continues that way. You're most welcome here. Now what'll you all be having?"

"I've got the first round," Jeremy said, the bad football match apparently a distant memory now. "So Mandy, how did you cope this summer without us?" They walked together up to the bar.

"Let's find some seats," Arvine suggested. "What would you like to drink? Tell Ben and he'll go help Jeremy."

"How about one of those snowball things you talked about at dinner?" I said. "They sound like fun."

"Me too," Kathy added. "Julie, how about you?"

"I think I'll have a beer, thanks."

Arvine looked at Bob, who said he'd have a Guinness. "All right, Ben – add another snowball for me and we're well away."

"So what exactly is a snowball, Arvine? What are you getting us into?" I asked.

"It's made with Advocaat and lemonade, with a cherry on top."

I already knew what English lemonade was, thanks to Colin. But Advocaat? I'd never heard of this. "What's Advocaat?"

"It's made of egg yolks, vanilla, brandy, and sugar. Don't you have it in America?"

"Not that I know of. It sounds a little like eggnog."

"Oh, it's completely different and much nicer. I think you'll like it."

Ben and Jeremy returned from the bar carrying two round trays loaded with everybody's drinks. The snowballs looked very festive in their glasses garnished with a slice of orange and a maraschino cherry. "Cheers!" we all yelled as we raised our drinks.

"Oh wow, Arvine. This tastes great!" Kathy said as she tried her snowball.

The snowball was excellent. It was smooth, creamy, sweet, and lemony. This was the kind of drink that was dangerous. Sure, it looked innocent enough, with its pale yellow color and frothy top. But you'd certainly feel it after you'd had a few of them.

The music started and we realized that the evening's entertainment was being provided by a one-man band. He had the whole contraption set up: a keyboard and synthesizer in front of him, a small, foot-operated drum set at his side, and a harmonica that was attached to one of those harnesses you put around your neck, a la Bob Dylan. An older couple got up and started to dance.

About an hour into the set, the musician leaned into the microphone and announced, "I understand we have some special guests here tonight who've come all the way from across the pond. Here's something for them." To our delight, he launched into Don McLean's "American Pie," one-man-band style.

"I love this song!" Julie said, as we all sang along with the musician. I think we knew the words better than he did. It was hilarious: we'd just flown halfway around the world and were in a little pub in the middle of nowhere singing one of the greatest

American anthems of the 1970s with a roomful of total strangers. We finished the song to cheering and applause from everyone in the pub.

"Thanks everyone! We do weddings, too," Bob said as the musician walked up to the bar to take a break. "Hey you guys, what's that glass thing hanging over the bar?" He pointed to what looked like a gigantic bud vase tipped on its side. It rested on two brackets that were mounted to the molding above the bar.

"That's a yard," answered Hugh. "A lot of the pubs have them."

"What's it for?"

"You drink ale out of it. But it's tricky. Most beginners who try to drink a yard end up wearing it instead."

"I think I'll try that out." Before Hugh could stop him, Bob walked up to the barman and said, "Hey, can I do a yard?"

"Oh, Bob!" Arvine said as everyone near the bar started laughing and clapping. "Hugh, quick, tell him what to do." Meanwhile, the barman climbed onto a chair, lifted the yard off its brackets and dusted it off. He placed the yard on the floor between his feet and began to pour ale slowly into it until the large bulb at the bottom was full. A small crowd gathered to watch the fun.

"Right – Bob, are you listening?" Hugh said quickly. "You can't just drink out of the yard as if it's a pint glass. The trick is to turn the whole thing in your hand. You turn it 'round and 'round so the ale comes out slowly in a thin dribble. Otherwise it all comes rushing out at once and you'll be soaked."

"O.K., I've got it," Bob assured Hugh. The barman stepped

out from behind the bar and presented Bob with the yard. There were more cheers and yells. Bob gave everybody a thumbs-up.

"I have a feeling this is going to end badly," Julie said to Arvine.

"Well, it'll be entertaining, at least," Kathy said.

I wish I'd brought my camera. Bob started off all right, coached by Hugh at his side. We were all cheering him on. "Not bad for a first-timer!" someone shouted. But then Bob got overconfident; he raised the yard just a little too high and stopped twirling it for a moment. That was all it took; the ale in the bulb surged forward like a tidal wave and Bob was doused in an instant.

We couldn't stop laughing. Bob was a good sport as people came up and clapped him on the shoulders for giving it a try.

"You get an A for effort, Bob!" I said as he gave me an ale-soaked grin. Maybe he wasn't such a jerk after all.

"Hey, I'll bet if you wring out your T-shirt into a glass, you'll get a pint's worth!" suggested Julie.

Before we left the pub for the night, the musician honored us with an encore performance of "American Pie." I'm afraid it wasn't quite as impressive as our original performance, which I blamed mostly on the alcohol. On the walk back to campus I asked Arvine, "So were we still in Canterbury at the pub?"

"No, it's actually a small village called Rough Common," she said. "Did you enjoy the pub?"

"Sure! That place was great – I don't think they're going to forget us anytime soon, do you?"

"Oh no," Arvine giggled. "No risk of that. So what else does the university have planned for you before classes begin?"

"Well, I guess there's another trip tomorrow after breakfast. Leeds Castle – have you been?"

"Yes, it's really lovely – one of the prettiest places in Kent, I think. It has a moat. You'll be back in time for the Freshers' Fair, I expect? You won't want to miss that."

"I think – I remember seeing something about it. That's where you can find out about clubs and sports teams, right?"

"Yes, that's it. There will be tables staffed by everybody from the student newspaper to the squash club and the student union. It's a fun way to see what you'd like to get involved with while you're here."

Back home I was a reporter for *The Mount Holyoke News*, the college's paper, as well as an FCC-licensed DJ for WMHC-FM, the college's radio station. I was excited to see what else I could sign up for here at UKC.

After another, even more off-key butchering of "American Pie," we'd arrived at Keynes College and said our goodnights at the G-block staircase. After two years at a women's college, it was kind of neat and a little weird having guys living on the neighboring floors. As I unlocked my door to grab my stuff for the trek back down the hall to the bathroom, I saw that someone had slipped a note underneath while I'd been out. *Hope you had a fun night out*, it read. *Will come COLLECT you (not the other thing) tomorrow for dinner! See you then. – Colin*

Two days in, and I'd already made some friends, done some sightseeing, and experienced an honest-to-goodness English country pub. This was going to be a good year.

Another proper country pub.
This one is The Duck Inn, located in Pett Bottom, near Canterbury.

Chapter Seven

The next morning at breakfast, we were looking forward to the trip to Leeds Castle, but there was one formality to get through first: an orientation session and security meeting for the American students. I knew there'd be some boring stuff — the first few days couldn't be all fun and games. The coaches would be taking us to the castle shortly after orientation was over. Kathy, Julie, Bob, and I walked over to the Senate building, where we'd all been asked to gather with our passports and completed police registration forms in hand.

As we walked in, we were greeted by somebody from Rod Smithson's department. He handed each of us a sticker and asked us to write our name and our U.S. college or university on it. I'd hated these dorky getting-to-know-you events during orientation week at Mount Holyoke — I always felt like I was on the spot and had to come up with something really interesting to say. I preferred to just plunk down beside somebody in the dining hall and introduce myself, or start knocking on doors. But I supposed this set-up was a good idea for people who were on the shyer side.

Just because they were so huge, the University of California, USC, UMass, and Indiana University systems were pretty well represented. There seemed to be lots of students from there. But as I walked around the room and started reading people's name tags, I also saw there were people from Notre Dame, Lehigh, Emory, Florida State, and Syracuse.

"Hi Diane!" someone called from nearby. It was Kerri, one of the Mount Holyoke students. I recognized her from a couple of classes we'd had together at home; we were both

English majors.

"Oh, hey Kerri. So which college did they put you in?"

"Eliot – what about you?"

"I'm in Keynes, the college with the duck pond. I had lunch in Eliot yesterday."

"Kind of a bummer to have to put on real clothes for breakfast, isn't it?"

"No kidding," I groaned. One of my favorite things about the Mount Holyoke dorms was that they were so homelike, no matter how old or new they were. There was always a large living room, a TV room, lots of smaller lounges, and a dining room in every dorm. Most people came downstairs to breakfast in their pajamas and slippers, unless they needed to get to an early morning class. I hadn't realized how much I loved that tradition until my first breakfast at UKC. Since I had to walk across an outdoor quad and halfway through Keynes just to get upstairs to the dining hall, there would be no bathrobes and bunny slippers at mealtimes in England.

"So have you met any of the other Mount Holyoke students who are here?" Kerri asked.

"Honestly, no." Before I left the States, I'd been given a list of my fellow MHC-ers with their names and photographs. I'd been so busy since arriving that I hadn't found the time to look them up.

"Come on over and say hi to everybody." Kerri led me up to three other women who I didn't even recognize. The first one Kerri introduced me to was Courtney, a serious-looking girl who quietly mentioned that she was on MHC's riding team.

"Oh wow – you are so lucky. So what do you think about it

here so far, Courtney?" I said.

"I hate it," was the quick reply. Her eyes filled up with tears. "I miss the stables and all of my friends on the riding team. The dorms here are so ugly. I didn't think it was going to be so...modern. And there doesn't seem to be much security here. I don't feel safe."

This last comment of Courtney's threw me; at Mount Holyoke, the whole safety thing had been drilled into us, I guess. The college, although small, had a beautiful, spread-out campus with plenty of wooded spaces and two lakes. It only made sense for all of us to be aware of our surroundings, especially when we were walking around campus late at night.

In some of the more remote parts of Mount Holyoke's campus there were emergency phones marked with bright blue lights. If you ever felt like you were in danger, you just ran to the phone, took the receiver off the hook, and the campus police would arrive in seconds. There was even a security van that made regular loops around campus so that you didn't have to walk anywhere late at night by yourself.

Our dorms at Mount Holyoke were pretty secure, too; you needed a key to get in, and all doors on the first floor were locked from the inside at all times of the day and night. There was usually a student "sitting bells" at the front reception desk (the "bell desk") in each dorm – if you didn't have a key and you wanted to get in, you had to ring the doorbell and wait for the person sitting bells to let you in.

But now that I was away from Mount Holyoke and its extra security measures, did I feel unsafe here, as Courtney claimed to be? I didn't think so. Sure, Keynes and Eliot Colleges were built on an open plan – just like the other two colleges were, too, I supposed. You didn't have to walk through the Porter's office to gain access to the rest of Keynes College, and the only doors that locked were those for our study bedrooms and the bathrooms, of course.

But this campus was brightly lit at night. I didn't think being on a co-ed campus was any less safe than being on a single-sex one. I got the feeling that since she'd arrived in Canterbury, Courtney had been spending a lot of time by herself in her room.

I felt sorry for her – she looked really homesick, lost, and sad. "I'll bet we have lots of fun once classes start, Courtney," I tried. "Why don't you have dinner with my friends and me tonight? I've met a bunch of English and American students and they're really cool. We've already been out to the pubs a couple of times."

"O.K. – sure."

Also in the small Mount Holyoke contingent here were Heidi and Keisha, both pretty brunettes who studied chemistry and politics, respectively, back at Mount Holyoke. And both completely unknown to me. We had a good laugh about the fact that none of us knew each other back home and had to come all the way to England to meet. You'd think that on Mount Holyoke's campus of about 2,000 students, we'd have bumped into each other once in a while. But each of us had different majors (aside from Kerri and me), separate groups of friends, and lived in different dorms that were scattered all over campus.

"Looks like the meeting is about to start," said Kerri. As we all scrambled for seats, one of Rod Smithson's people began to speak.

"Well good morning, everybody – I know you're eager to see Leeds Castle, so we'll keep this as brief as we can. Just some police formalities to deal with." He motioned to two officers who'd just stepped into the auditorium. "These gentlemen are here from the constabulary in Canterbury. It's important that we get you registered with the constabulary as being short-stay students from abroad. By having information such as your passport numbers on file with the authorities, we'll have all of your details handy in the event of an emergency."

"Well, that's a downer," said Kerri.

One by one, we all lined up so the police officers could copy down our passport numbers and take our registration forms. Then they gave our passports a special stamp that said we had registered with the authorities.

"That's it?" I asked the officer.

"That's it," he said with a smile.

"The coaches to Leeds Castle are waiting outside," Rod Smithson's guy said. "As soon as you're finished here, you can board a coach."

The trip to Leeds Castle was a fun day out, and the castle certainly was a monumental building, with its large moat and expansive lawns. But in my book, it just couldn't compare with beautiful Canterbury Cathedral. I knew where I'd be spending a lot of my spare time.

"So what's going on when we get back?" Julie asked me on the ride back from Leeds.

"It's the Freshers' Fair. We can sign up for sports and clubs and stuff. Are you going?"

"No, I think I'll pass. Unless they have a running club. Maybe I'd join that."

"Kathy, do you want to come to the Fair with me?"

"Sure – I don't know if I'll join anything, but I'll go check it out with you."

When the coaches pulled into Keynes, we ran back to our rooms to dump our things and then headed straight over to Rutherford College. The Freshers' Fair was set up in the dining hall. Around the perimeter of the hall were dozens of tables staffed by students who represented all of the university's organizations. Large placards on the walls behind each table announced the name of the organization.

"Oh wow, I didn't think it would be this big," Kathy said. "There's tons of stuff to look at here. What are you interested in?"

"I don't know. Something really different that I'd never do at home. And something that'll help us meet English students. Let's just walk around and see what there is."

We passed the Amnesty International table, which had some sullen-looking people passing out political pamphlets showing prisoners of conscience in foreign countries. "They look like a fun crowd," Kathy cracked.

There was a vegan society, chess club, taekwondo club, debating society, and something called a squash club. "O.K., I have to know what squash is," I said as I led Kathy over. "Oh, check it out – it's like badminton!"

"No, it's not like badminton at all," the skinny student at

the table said as he glared at me.

"I have terrible hand-eye coordination anyway," I told him as we walked away laughing.

Then, across the room, I saw a brightly colored placard that read BALLROOM DANCING CLUB. "Kathy, look! They have a ballroom dancing club. What could be more English than that? I'll bet we meet tons of Brits that way. Come on!" We made our way over to the table and were greeted by two students who introduced themselves as Isabella and Noel (so English!).

"What can we tell you about the club?" Isabella asked. She was very regal-looking, with long, wavy hair and perfect posture. I could just picture her floating across a dance floor in a billowy dress like Ginger Rogers.

"Well, how often do you meet? And do you take beginners? We don't know a thing about ballroom dancing, except that it sounds like fun."

"Oh it is! It's ever so easy to learn. We meet every Monday night in Eliot College from 8 'til 10, and we learn everything from waltz and foxtrot to Latin dances like the cha-cha and samba," Isabella said.

Noel added, "We also go to lots of the local dance halls on a weekend so that we can dance in proper ballrooms. And if you're interested, you can even join a special team that enters inter-university ballroom dance competitions. You have to be in the advanced class for that."

"Don't scare them off, Noel!" Isabella said. "Would you like to have a go? We start this coming Monday – perfect way to end your first day of classes."

"What do you think, Kathy?" I asked. I'd already decided

I was in. There was nothing like this at Mount Holyoke. How cool would it be to learn ballroom dancing? My parents and grandparents were amazing dancers and they'd be so excited when I told them I was finally learning, too.

"O.K., count me in, too," Kathy said.

"Lovely!" Isabella beamed. "You're both going to have such fun. Just sign your names and colleges here. We'll see you Monday!"

"I'm so psyched, Kathy!" I said as we waved goodbye to Isabella and Noel. "I think we're going to have a blast. Let's see what else there is over here. Rugby club? God, I think I'd get killed... Radio station? I already do that at Mount Holyoke... Rowing club? I'm not very strong."

"But you are little – you could be a coxswain." The guy staffing the rowing club's table stood up and stuck out his hand. He was dark and stocky, with tightly curled hair and a thick accent that I couldn't place. "I am Amatsia. Our men's four needs a new cox. What do you know about rowing?"

I looked at the display on his table; it featured lots of photos of the university's boats and various team shots from different races they'd competed in. "Pretty much nothing," I admitted. But rowing did seem like an extremely English activity, too, just like ballroom dancing. Hey, I could even be like Rob Lowe in the movie *Oxford Blues*: American arrives on campus and takes the rowing club by storm.

"Ah, not important." Amatsia waved his hand dismissively. "We will teach you."

"I'm not sure. I'm only here for the year on an exchange program, and I want to travel a lot. I don't think I want to get

100

involved in something as serious as a sports team." The crew team back at Mount Holyoke was pretty intense. They got up at the crack of dawn and competed all over New England. I wanted to have a fun year here in England.

"No. No team –just a club. Only two practices a week, Wednesday afternoons and Saturday mornings. A few events a year, including The Boat Race on the Thames. You know The Boat Race, yes? Oxford against Cambridge?"

Of course I knew about The Boat Race – that was one of the big scenes at the end of *Oxford Blues*. Kathy elbowed me. "Oh, go ahead, Diane – you were just saying you wanted to do something really different."

"Yes, yes – listen to your friend. She is very smart." Amatsia put a pen in my hand. "Welcome to our new cox! We see you next Wednesday at 1pm in Eliot car park. It will be great fun."

"Uh, O.K., sure! My parents are going to die laughing when I tell them about this," I said to Kathy as I signed up. I looked at Amatsia. "What do I need to bring with me?"

"Nothing. Just your lovely small self." He paused briefly. "Oh – and some not-very-nice shoes. Maybe you will get muddy."

"Got it. Cruddy shoes. I'll be there."

"You did what?! Oh my God – this is going to be hysterical!" Julie laughed over dinner that night. "Do you know anything about rowing?"

"Not a thing!" I said. "But the guy who's the president made it kind of impossible to say no. You'll have to meet him – he's

101

quite a character."

"I think it's wonderful, Diane," Colin said. "Well done."

"Thank you, Colin. And I expect every one of you to come cheer me on at my first regatta as I cox the men's four to victory...or crash us into the riverbank, which is way more likely." We took up nearly a whole banquet table in the dining hall tonight: Arvine and her gang, Kathy, Julie, Bob, Colin, and me.

Courtney had even come out as she'd promised, but she sat silently at the table through the entire dinner, looking scared of her own shadow. We all took turns trying to pull her out of her shell, but didn't have much success. I personally didn't think she was going to last until Christmas, and neither did Kathy. Even if she did, by some chance, I doubted she'd be coming back to England after the Christmas break. She'd told us that she'd be flying back to the States for Christmas, whereas most of the Americans had decided to stay in England and go travelling.

"All right, who's up for a pint in the Keynes bar?" Hugh asked as we all got up to return our dinner trays to the carts. "Let's toast Diane's new athletic endeavour. No yards for you tonight, Bob – you need some more training."

✧ Chapter Eight ✧

I couldn't believe how quickly my first six weeks had flown. Most of my classes were pretty interesting, which was good, considering I'd be stuck with them for the entire year. Unlike American colleges, where you started new courses at the beginning of the second semester, UKC had one long year divided into three terms, but you kept the same four courses across those terms.

I was taking Shakespeare and Related Drama, Eighteenth-Century Studies, French Poets Since Baudelaire, and French Romanticism. My favorite class so far was Eighteenth-Century Studies. It was a popular class — so big, in fact, that the weekly lectures were held in a huge auditorium, concert-style. Several professors took turns leading the lectures. Once a week, we all broke into smaller seminars where we were assigned to a specific professor.

The course material ranged from the plays of Alexander Pope and Samuel Johnson's *Dictionary* to the engravings of Hogarth and the works of Jonathan Swift. We even studied the music and building styles of eighteenth-century composers and architects. I loved it, because there was something different for every lecture or seminar.

One of the professors who regularly took a turn at the large weekly lectures was especially popular with the American girls. His name was Thomas Erving, and he was incredibly dashing. He had enormous sideburns and a booming, dramatic speaking voice; I could easily picture him on the stage of a theater in London's West End. He rolled his "r's" in the most amazing way. It was very cool. We loved when it was his turn to lecture.

Once the weather started getting colder, Mr. Erving began wearing a tweed cloak and matching cap that made him look an awful lot like Sherlock Holmes. The effect was striking. He rode his bicycle everywhere and almost always had a pipe sticking out of his mouth. You could always tell when he was late, because he'd be pedaling furiously with his cloak billowing out behind him in a brown, tweedy cloud.

My seminar leader for Eighteenth-Century Studies was this crazy professor named Ranulph Frampton. We'd pack into his fantastically disorganized office once a week and have a lively, interesting discussion about a given theme. Then, if time allowed, which it did more often than not, we'd be treated to what we secretly called a "Ranulph Rant" on whatever was pissing him off that week. It frequently had to do with the English royal family, whom he hated with a passion.

"Parasites, every last one of them," he'd bluster. "Just think of all the taxpayer money they get from the Civil List[2]." I was dying to point out to Mr. Frampton that whatever money the royal family received from the Civil List was probably far exceeded by the tourist income that they generated – especially from all of the Americans who headed straight to attractions like The Tower of London, Buckingham Palace, and Windsor Castle. But Ranulph Frampton in a rage was a wondrous spectacle to behold, and it was fun to watch him get all self-righteous and worked up into full throttle.

Life in Canterbury was falling into a very enjoyable rhythm.

---

[2] The Civil List is the money that the British government sets aside to pay the royals their salaries, for lack of a better word.

Most days after class I'd try to get my work done early, so that I could hang out with my friends in the evening. It was a nice change from Mount Holyoke, where I'd typically study late into the nights during the week. Some nights it was just Julie, Kathy, Bob, and me getting together in somebody's room. Other nights we'd join Arvine, Ben, Jeremy, and Hugh at The Dog and Bear, where we were now known collectively as "Arvine and her Yanks." Sometimes Colin would join us, and sometimes I would go places with just him.

Kathy and I were having a blast at ballroom dancing – it had quickly become one of the highlights of our week. Our initial hunch about ballroom dancing being a great way to meet English students was right on; there were only a few Americans in the club. Every Monday night after dinner, we'd walk together over to Eliot and spend the next two hours or so laughing at how awful we were, and marveling at how smoothly Noel and Isabella glided over the floor.

Our instructor was a compact British woman named Barbara – we promptly nicknamed her "Babs." She was an accomplished ballroom dancer, and she didn't put up with any crap. For the two hours that we were in the Eliot dining hall, she owned us. I wasn't prepared for how much of a workout we'd be getting, but one look at Babs's calves was proof; the muscle definition in them was incredible. Every single Monday, she wore the same strappy, gold high heels. I, meanwhile, struggled to get my steps right in my sensible, gray, low-heeled shoes.

Babs brought a boom box and her own music with her. She always opened every Monday's session with the same warm-up song: the classic "I Won't Dance." We loved the irony. People would find their partners and start whirling around the floor. Once the song ended, the formal instruction would begin.

Babs was such a kick-ass dancer that she was able to teach the men's *and* the ladies' parts to us. First she'd have all the guys line up behind her in a single row. Noel and one of the other guys in the advanced class would be on her right or left to help out. Then she'd coach the row of guys through their steps a few times, having them do the same behind her. Leaving Noel and his assistant to keep drilling the guys, Babs would then do the same with us ladies – Isabella and one of her friends would step forward to help. Once Babs was happy with our progress, we paired up with our partners and made a few trips around the floor.

My first partner was David, an English boy from Keynes. I took an instant dislike to him because he was a sexist pig. Babs assigned our partners to us on the first night that the club met; she explained that the ideal ballroom dancing silhouette was one where the man was exactly one head taller than the woman. David and I fit the bill and happened to be standing near each other that first night, so we ended up together. Luckily, Babs would have us switch partners a couple of times each Monday, so we'd get to know different styles of leading and meet the other students in the club.

By the end of our sixth week, we had all made measurable progress and could perform a halfway decent quickstep (my best dance), as well as a pretty good waltz, cha-cha, and bossanova. Babs announced that we had done so well that she felt we were ready to dance in public. At the very end of

November, there would be a ball at the King's Hall in Herne Bay. If we wanted to sign up and buy our tickets ahead of time, she'd arrange to hire a coach to take us there and back.

The rowing club was going equally well. Despite my nervousness about being completely out of my comfort zone, I was having a great time. Amatsia, our club's de facto captain, was a wild man. I learned that he was a post-grad student; his studies involved some kind of lab science that I tried to very hard to understand without much success. He held an Israeli passport, spoke French, English, and Hebrew, and had a mouth like a truck driver. But he had a great sense of humor, which was made all the more funny by his heavy accent and not-quite-thorough grasp of the English language.

With my total lack of rowing and coxing experience, I figured I'd be a liability to the men's four, but Amatsia assured me that I'd be a success. "You arc little but loud," he said. "This is because you are American. Everyone will hear you. Your stroke will teach you what to scream. Just scream what he says to scream." I nodded dumbly and hoped everything would turn out O.K. – I gathered that a stroke was one of the guys who'd be in the boat with me.

If anybody had told me back at Mount Holyoke that I'd be sitting in a boat on the River Stour in England and in charge of four men, I would've laughed myself silly. But here I was, and it was terrific fun. My stroke was a guy named Ian who also lived in Keynes College. He'd gone to a swanky private school for boys in Portsmouth, on the south coast of England, and he'd been in his school's rowing club – except they rowed on the open ocean! He was patient with me, and carefully explained all of the finer points of coxing to me, including all of the calls I'd need to learn.

"O.K. dumb question," I asked at the rowing club's first outing. "Why are you called a stroke?"

"Not a dumb question at all," Ian assured me. "I set the stroke, or the pace, for the boat. You steer and tell us what to do. The other lads watch my blade and they keep pace with how fast and deep it moves. Since you can see everybody, you shout out their seat positions and correct their form. Don't worry, I'll tell you what to yell until you get sorted."

Say what?
Brit/Yank Translator

Blade: *oar*

"Steer the boat?! I don't even have my driver's license at home! What if I crash this thing?"

"Then we'll have to change its name from the *Kentish Hops* to the *Titanic*, I reckon. I'm just having fun – we won't let you sink the boat."

My first outing on the river was memorable, to say the least. The stretch of the Stour where the university's club rowed was pretty narrow in some spots, and in the beginning it must've looked to any spectators like we were playing bumper boats. Eventually, as Ian promised, I did start getting the hang of it and gaining more confidence.

Sometimes Amatsia would take a spot in one of the men's fours or eights, but he usually preferred to row on his own. After only our fifth or sixth practice, we returned to the boathouse to find him standing on the landing slip looking dazed and holding his head in his hands. When we asked him what was wrong, he shook his head and answered in his thickly accented English, "Ah, it is not a good day – I cracked my skull."

"What!?" I yelled to Ian. "He's being awfully blasé for someone with a head injury. Shouldn't we call an ambulance or something?"

At this, Amatsia's face creased up in laughter as he choked out, "Oh my little Di-ah-na. You make me laugh. Not the skull of my head. The scull that is the boat for one person. Ha ha ha!"

My favorite part of the rowing club was the Saturday morning practice, because it featured the rowing equivalent of après ski. After we finished practice, wiped down the boats, and put them away in the boathouse, we'd pile into everyone's cars and head for The Gate Inn – a fabulous country pub that was more or less on the drive back to the university. It would be lunchtime by then, so we'd all have a pint of something and one of the pub's famous "Cheesy Gateburgers" with loads of chips fresh out of the deep-fat fryer.

There was almost always a roaring fire going in The Gate's fireplace, and the pub had beautiful garlands of dried hops – used to brew beer – decorating the old, exposed wooden beams along the ceiling. It was a cozy, warm place to spend a lazy afternoon, which is usually what ended up happening once we'd arrived there in our damp and muddy rowing clothes.

Six weeks into my junior year abroad, I'd also made quite a few day trips and done lots of interesting things. On one of my

109

first trips outside Canterbury, Kerri and I spent the day in Dover, famous for its white cliffs, Tudor castle, and ferry port. A bunch of us had also gone back to the cathedral for choral evensong and for classical concerts performed by visiting orchestras. We'd been to see some plays at Canterbury's Marlowe Theatre, too.

The entertainment on campus wasn't too shabby, either. UKC had its own performance theatre called The Gulbenkian and, since our arrival, we'd been to a couple of plays and two live concerts there. The university had an extremely well respected dramatic and theatre arts program, so the rest of the students benefited from that – there was always some major musical act or theatre production coming through, in addition to the plays and musicals put on by the university's own dramatic group. All in all, there wasn't a lack of things to do. Most of us Americans were settling in nicely, with one exception.

Kathy and I had been right about Courtney – she didn't even make it to Thanksgiving. She'd gotten increasingly homesick and sad, despite our attempts to help her. Colin had made it his special mission to take her around campus and into Canterbury, and we figured that if anybody could get Courtney out of her funk, Colin could. But even his attentions hadn't helped. In mid-November, Courtney packed her bags and got on a plane back to the U.S. and Mount Holyoke, which she probably never should've left in the first place.

Coxing into the sunset – definitely more fun (and scenic) than studying in the library.

Dealing With Culture Shock

It's a completely normal part of the study abroad experience. But luckily, culture shock is usually never severe enough to make you cut your year short. That said, it's handy to be familiar with the different stages as you go through them.

Think of the beginning of your year abroad as the honeymoon stage – you've just arrived on your new campus and everything is fascinating, fun, new, and exciting. After a while, though, you start getting annoyed by little things: the way the food is cooked, for example, or the type of clothes the local students wear. Maybe it's something as silly as the weather or the bus schedule.

During this stage, you might feel a little hostile towards your new surroundings. Perhaps you start second-guessing your decision to spend a year abroad. When you feel like this, it's important to reassure yourself that things in your new country aren't supposed to be like home. That's why you decided to go abroad, after all.

You'll probably move onto the next stage without even realizing it. Before you know it, you've accepted the idiosyncrasies, settled into a routine, made some good friends, and begun to think of your host country as a second home. Finally, as the end of your junior year approaches, you'll feel so at home that you might be sad or nervous about returning to the United States. And guess what? That's completely normal, too.

✧ Chapter Nine ✧

Courtney's departure got us to thinking about home; back in America, Thanksgiving would be coming soon. Of course, over here it would be just like any other day – although the university had arranged to cater a special Thanksgiving dinner in the evening for any American students who were feeling a little homesick (or for English students who were feeling a little curious).

But Kathy, Julie, Bob, and I had other plans for the holiday. We had decided to cook a traditional Thanksgiving dinner with all of the trimmings for our English friends. We just needed a real kitchen. Luckily, we'd gotten to know Mike, one of Arvine's friends and a fellow student who lived off campus and rented a house in a development near the university. When we told Mike about our idea, he happily loaned us his kitchen. There would be quite a crowd to cook for: 11 of us, and as far as I knew, none of my American friends had attempted to cook anything on such a grand scale.

My mom is a fantastic cook, but also a traditional Italian mom – the kitchen is her domain. At home, I'd lend a hand by washing pots and pans or loading the dishwasher, but that's where my culinary expertise ended. Kathy, Julie, and Bob weren't exactly domestic geniuses, either. We wanted to do something special for our English friends to thank them for making us feel so welcome in their country, and we didn't want them to do any work. If we were going to pull off this feat and not give anybody food poisoning, we were going to need some serious phone time with our moms.

Over the next week or so, the four of us planned the menu and decided who would be in charge of preparing each dish. Then we called home for advice. We felt reasonably confident about the easy stuff like mashed potatoes and veggies, but we were a little nervous about the stuffing and turkey. I'd heard horror stories about people who accidentally left the stuffing inside the turkey for a while and then served it later, giving their guests botulism, salmonella, or something equally gross.

Cranberries were a worry, too. Could we even get whole berries or canned sauce over here? We'd have to make sure we allowed enough time for someone at home to mail us a can or two in case we came up with nothing at the grocery store. Pies were also a big unknown. Would we able to find pumpkin pie filling on the store shelves? It was time for a reconnaissance trip to the Sainsbury's supermarket.

I don't know what we looked like to the English shoppers as we spread out through the grocery store. I'm sure they thought we were all a little odd. We each had a list of ingredients that we needed for our own recipes, and a victory shout would go up from different parts of the store whenever we found an item that we'd doubted would be there.

Kathy and I actually climbed up to scour the tops and backs of the shelves in the canned fruit and veggie aisles – much to our surprise, we found a single can of cranberry sauce and some forlorn-looking cans of pumpkin pie filling. We snatched those up right away and saved the rest of the grocery shopping for right before Thanksgiving.

One cool thing about spending Thanksgiving outside America? Being able to go to the grocery store the day before the holiday without crowds, mayhem, and chaos in the aisles and parking lot. If you've ever forgotten that one critical ingredient the day before Thanksgiving and have had to run out to get it late that afternoon, you know exactly what I'm talking about.

The day before Thanksgiving in the Canterbury Sainsbo's, though, was a breeze. The four of us sailed along almost empty aisles, happily tossing stuff in our shopping carts and crossing things off our lists. We were almost giddy with excitement. Our poor moms would've have been insanely jealous. We headed back to Mike's flat and stuffed his small fridge to the bursting point.

On Thanksgiving Day, Kathy, Julie, Bob, and I blew off our classes and headed over to Mike's to start cooking. We'd had our final coaching sessions with our moms last night and were ready to snap into action. We had a boom box and a stack of Kathy's George Winston tapes to keep us company while we worked. Our English friends would be arriving later in the afternoon, and had been kind enough to chip in a little money to help defray the cost of the shopping trip. Everybody was excited.

The dinner was a huge success; nobody got sick from undercooked turkey, we remembered to take the stuffing out of the bird before we served dinner, the veggies were crisp and American-style, and the pies were not burnt. We'd even made a huge punchbowl of snowballs to serve as before-dinner drinks.

The only moment of panic came when we took the turkey

out of the oven and set it on the countertop. "So who wants the honor of carving?" one of us asked. We all automatically looked at Bob – since carving was a dad thing and Bob was a guy, we figured he was the logical choice.

"Don't look at me," he said. "My dad does all that stuff."

We couldn't believe it – in all the calls back home, we'd completely forgotten to ask how to carve the turkey! We couldn't call the mom hotline now; the phone in Mike's flat took incoming calls only. Arvine ended up saving the day and doing the honors.

When dinner was over, our English friends asked, "What do we do now?"

Julie started laughing. "Now we all fall asleep in front of the TV until it's time to wake up for dessert! Then we have leftovers for the next three days."

There was no Macy's Thanksgiving Day parade or post-dinner American football game to watch on the TV, of course, but Hugh did manage to find a soccer match. "Will that do?" he asked as we planted ourselves on the floor, the chairs, and the couch. "It is called 'football' over here, after all."

"Hugh, that's perfect," I said.

And it was. Thanksgiving of 1986 – my first one away from my country, family, and childhood friends – was the best one I'd ever had.

One of the American students that year wrote a poem that captured everyone's mood perfectly. She had made copies and shared them with all of the other Americans on campus. It was titled, simply, "Thanksgiving Poem" and it read:

116

Take an empty suitcase
Put your life inside
Ship it off to England
Family, friends, goodbye.

Strange places lie before us
New accents in our ears.
Fixing up our rooms
We might just like it here.

Meeting lots of people
Choosing a new class
Drink another lager
Gosh, I hope I pass.

At 10 another lecture
Just like ones at home
Study break at two
With tea and maybe scones.

Allow five hours for laundry
Queues in no great hurry
Just in time for dinner
Lamb, prawns, chips, or curry?

Calling home with pounds in hand
Sometimes it's a pain
Ask Mom for more money
Describe the wind and rain

All here now together
With friends as family
Laughing, drinking, talking
Eating pie and roast turkey.

But especially today
We remember why we're here
We thank God for the gifts He gives
Today and throughout the year.

✧ Chapter Ten ✧

If my first six weeks went quickly, the next six were a blur. Right after our successful Thanksgiving dinner, the ballroom dancing club was unleashed on an unsuspecting public on its first official outing to the King's Hall in Herne Bay. We had a huge turnout. There were so many of us, in fact, that we filled the entire coach.

I now had a new partner – an English guy named Kevin. Things with David hadn't worked out so well and we'd both decided that we'd be better off with new partners. I think I was probably getting on his nerves as much as he was getting on mine. An assertive woman and a sexist pig don't make such a good combination. The last straw was when David had invited me up to his room for a coffee one Monday night after practice.

Know Before You Go

When Coffee is NOT Coffee

What's so bad about someone asking if you'd like a coffee? Here's where cultural differences rear their ugly little heads again. Before I'd left Mount Holyoke for England, Allison had warned me that there was a distinct difference between an English boy inviting you back to his room for tea, and one who was inviting you back to his room for a coffee.

"Tea means just that," she'd said knowingly. "A cup of tea. But a coffee means something else. And it's most definitely not coffee."

119

"Oh, wow – you mean he's looking to fool around with you?" I'd said.

"Exactly. So make sure you know what – or whom – is on the menu!" We had shrieked with laughter.

As far as I was concerned, David was not my coffee type. And he wasn't my cup of tea, either. So we told Babs that we needed new partners if we were both going to stay in the club. Luckily, a guy had just dropped out of the club, leaving a girl stranded. Problem solved for David, but I was still on my own. Babs looked around. "Hang on, Diane – I think one of our young men has just lost his partner, as well. Yes, there he is. Kevin, come over here and meet your new partner, dear!"

A slender, dark-haired guy across the dining hall detached himself from his group of friends and laughed loudly as he strode away from them. He broke into a whistle as he confidently walked up to Babs and me with his head tilting from side to side in time to the tune he was whistling. My first impression was that this guy was stuck on himself.

My second impression was that it looked as if his jeans had been painted on; they were the skin-tight Pepe brand that were all the rage with the English, and they left absolutely nothing to the imagination. I'd gone straight from the frying pan and into the fire. Wasn't there somebody else I could dance with?

Before I knew it, though, Babs had put me in Kevin's arms in the ready position for a quickstep. Then she stood back and took a long, admiring look at us. "Oh, that's lovely – a perfect silhouette. That's just gorgeous." Pleased with her work, Babs clicked away in her strappy gold heels and began to play our warm-up dance.

"Hi, I'm Kevin," he said matter-of-factly as we began our first trip around the floor. "Well, that was a bit of luck. My partner just quit on me."

"I'm Diane. My first partner and I couldn't stand each other. He's over there." I turned my head around to where David was standing awkwardly with his new partner.

"Ladies, please – heads back and eyes over the gentlemen's shoulders," Babs coached. She glared at me.

"Oh, him," Kevin frowned as we whirled by David. "He's a bit of a wet fart – he lives on my block at Keynes."

"A wet fart? What the hell is that?"

"You know – not much fun."

"You've got that right. And he tried to get me back to his room for a coffee last week. I don't think my boyfriend back at home would've been too excited about that." I threw that last comment in there just in case Mr. Tight Pants was getting any ideas of his own.

"I've got someone back at home, too – haven't seen her in a couple of weeks. I suppose your boyfriend is back in America, then?"

Good, he had someone already. "Yes – it's kind of complicated." Now I was afraid I'd come off as a little bitchy to Kevin. He was just making polite conversation, and I had to admit he was a good leader – much better than David was. Whereas David's grip on my hand was half-hearted and sweaty, Kevin's was firm. And he wasn't afraid to put pressure on the small of my back with his other hand and steer me around the floor.

121

It was a lot easier to dance with a guy who could lead confidently. Even if his pants were way too tight.

The ball at Herne Bay was a success. Babs was so excited by our performance that she proposed we make it a monthly-ish treat. We were at least 20 years younger than everyone else in King's Hall, and the "grannies and granddads," as Kevin called them, got a real kick out of watching a bunch of university students show off their stuff. A few of them gave us nods of approval or polite comments like "well done" as they danced past us. At the very end of the evening, after the last dance, everyone in the hall stood to attention and faced the compere.

Say what?

Brit/Yank Translator

Compere: *the emcee of a ballroom dancing event who announces the name of each song and which kind of dance it is (e.g., Viennese waltz, tango, polka, etc.)*

"What are we all doing?" I asked Kevin. Everyone else seemed to know what was going on.

"We're standing for the Queen, of course," he replied. The National Anthem began to play and everyone started to sing. It was kind of like being at Fenway Park for a Red Sox game, except the Brits did their song at the end instead of as an opener. I noticed that one of Kevin's friends was deliberately silent. "Oh, that's just Jon being bloody-minded," Kevin remarked. "He's from the North, you see. They don't like the royal family up there. No respect for our sovereign."

On the coach ride back, I sat with Kevin and some of his friends. They were all in Keynes College, except they were over in C Block, near the Porter's Lodge and the bank of pay phones I used to make my weekly calls to Sal and my parents.

"Our rooms overlook the car park," Kevin said. "Not much of a view. Don't you have the duck pond over in G Block?"

"No, that's F Block — but the ducks are always walking over to G Block's quad. That's because we feed them from our bedroom windows. It's pretty funny."

"So what are your plans for Christmas break, then, Diane? I hear that all you Americans are packing up your rucksacks and travelling once classes end. We have a couple of American blokes on our corridor. Eric — the one who does the bodybuilding competitions. Maybe you know him?"

"I do. And I think I know another American on your corridor. Eric's friend William — he's in the rowing club with me."

"Oh yes! William's good fun. So you row?"

"Oh God, no — I'm just the designated yeller. I'm the cox for one of the men's fours. Do you do any sports here?"

"Squash and football, mostly — and I'm in the university's skydiving club. You should come see us do a jump sometime."

"Skydiving! Weren't you petrified the first time you jumped? I could never do that."

"It's the most amazing feeling in the world," Kevin said. "It's even better than sex." He winked and smiled as I gaped in shock. Once again, so much for British reserve. At the very least, Kevin would be a far more entertaining partner than David ever was. Ballroom dancing had just gotten way more fun.

✧ Chapter Eleven ✧

December had begun, and Christmas break would be coming soon. All of the American students were firming up their travel plans or putting the finishing touches on their itineraries. Some of us, like Kathy and me, were using the break as an opportunity to explore the United Kingdom at greater length than we could on weekends.

Others, like Bob, were going really far away; he'd planned an adventurous trip that included a long stay in Egypt. I was envious, but surprised when I heard about all the shots he'd needed to get, plus the malaria pills that he'd have to take while he was there. Still, it was a place that I wanted to see eventually, despite my dread of needles.

Kathy and I were pretty psyched about our coming trip. The plan was to meet up at Arvine's house after Christmas, where we'd celebrate New Year's. Then we'd take the train to Carlisle, which was a good base for exploring parts of Hadrian's Wall. From there, we'd train it to Scotland, where we'd visit Edinburgh and Glasgow. A brief visit to Belfast, Northern Ireland, via ferry was next, followed by the Republic of Ireland, where we'd visit Dublin, Cork, and Blarney.

The final leg of the trip would be a ferry ride back to Wales, where we'd catch the train to London and stay a couple of days. From there, it was only a short train ride back to Canterbury. We'd be travelling on a shoestring, backpacking and staying mostly in youth hostels to keep the costs down, but we'd budgeted for a stay in a bed and breakfast here and there. Even better, I wouldn't have to spend money on a backpack; Colin was going to let me borrow his.

Colin already told me that I could store my things in his Parkwood flat on campus during the Christmas break and stay there as long as I liked after classes broke up for the holidays – we had to vacate our rooms by December 17th, so we couldn't leave anything in them during Christmas vacation like we did at Mount Holyoke.

In the meantime, though, there were still a lot of things left on the social calendar, the first one being the rowing club's Christmas party (at The Gate, of course). The night after that was the United Nations Association's (UNA) Ball – the university's social event of the year. It was a formal, with gowns or cocktail dresses and tuxedos required.

It hadn't occurred to me that I might be going to an event like this while in England. Fortunately, I'd found out about it far enough in advance that my mom was able to ship my favorite semi-formal dress from home. It was fire-engine red and very Audrey Hepburn, with a red net overskirt that had polka dots all over it, a flouncy tulle underskirt, a wide, red satin sash that tied in the back, spaghetti straps, and matching wrap.

The UNA Ball was elegant and festive, and the university pulled out all the stops for this one: covered walkways between all of the colleges so that nobody had to worry about bad weather spoiling their clothes; a multi-course dinner catered by an outside firm; bottles of wine at all the tables; blue and gold decorations everywhere; a string quartet that played during dinner; and a fantastic DJ for dancing afterward. It wasn't like a prom, so we didn't need dates – I ended up going with all of my English ballroom dancing club friends, since my American friends and Arvine's gang weren't interested. They missed a great night.

In addition to parties and balls, we even managed to squeeze in a couple of nice dinners at restaurants in Canterbury to celebrate Hugh's 21st and Bob's 22nd birthdays. One of the things I was getting to love about going out to eat in restaurants over here was the famous Student Discount. At most restaurants in Canterbury, you got some kind of break when you showed your Student Union ID card or UKC photo ID. The discount varied and was entirely at the management's discretion. Sometimes it was a free dessert for everybody, sometimes it was a free bottle of the house wine, and sometimes it was a flat discount off your bill.

The very last thing we did as a group before everyone began leaving for Christmas break was to attend the university's caroling service at the cathedral. I'd been looking forward to it, since I'd first heard about it in October. As it turned out, getting there ended up being half the fun, as the saying goes.

Rather than wait for the red double-decker buses, a bunch of us piled into Kevin's shiny, mustard-yellow Mini and headed into Canterbury. This was long before the cars were available for sale in America, so I'd never seen them before, except in the movies.

If you've never been in an original English Mini, this car gives the word "subcompact" a whole new meaning. The interior consisted of two bucket seats up front and a small back seat. Somehow we managed to cram six people, including Kevin, into his Mini. I was actually lying across the laps of the people in the back seat. The poor car was practically dragging on the ground, and we all held our breath with every speed bump. When we arrived at the cathedral and began to spill out of the Mini, it must've looked like a clown car from a circus.

The caroling service was out of this world. The entire cathedral was lit only by the flames of the hundreds of tapers that each one of us was given as we entered. Folding chairs packed the entire length of the nave except for a small aisle that ran down the middle; those of us who couldn't find seats parked ourselves on the shallow stairs that led up to the altar. From this perch, we looked out across the entire candlelit cathedral. It was absolutely gorgeous.

The program for the night alternated between songs performed by the university's various chorales and musical groups, and songs that all of us sang together, caroling-style. Kathy and I noticed that the English tune for "Away in a Manger" was entirely different from the American one, although the words were the same. And we both fell in love with an English carol that was new to us: "Once in Royal David's City." I was seated between Kathy and Kevin, and couldn't help but hear Kevin's beautiful singing voice.

"I used to be a choir boy in my church at home in Petersfield," he admitted, when I complimented him on his voice. "And yes, I wore the ruffled neck collar and long robe."

After the caroling service was over, we all headed back to Kevin's room for biscuits and tea (not coffee). Eventually, we said our goodbyes and made our ways back to our rooms; most of us still hadn't begun to pack up our things for the long Christmas break.

It was past midnight when I heard a knock at my door. Kevin was standing there with a Christmas card for me and a large, handled shopping bag at his side. I let him in and then eagerly opened the card, which had two little English robins on the front (I later learned that these cute, pudgy birds are associated with Christmas over here). Inside, Kevin had written: *Hope you have a great Christmas and fantastic time touring this lovely country of ours, and that you don't miss America and Sal too much. xoxo Kevin*

Of course, packing went out the window for the next hour or so, while Kevin and I talked and talked about our plans for the holidays. Since the night when Babs had paired us up at ballroom dancing, I'd gotten to know Kevin much better, and I was embarrassed that I'd judged him so harshly based on that first impression. It was time to 'fess up, and I sheepishly told him what I'd thought the first time I saw him in his too-tight Pepe jeans. He laughed and admitted he'd done exactly the same thing with me.

"Well, fair is fair, I reckon. I thought *you* were a boring little priss with your long denim skirt, old lady shoes, and that frilly-collar blouse," he said. This was 1986, remember – Lady Diana and her clown-collar, puffy-sleeved blouses were still all the rage at home in the States, and I was very much on the preppy side anyway.

Then Kevin said, "I wanted to show you something. I got this for Caroline for Christmas. Do you think she'll like it?" He pulled a shallow, shrink-wrapped basket from the shopping bag and held it out for me to inspect. It was a beautiful selection of shower gels, soaps, and lotions from The Body Shop, which had quickly become one of my favorite stores since I'd arrived in England. Every couple of weeks or so, I'd go into town and treat myself to one of their glycerin bars. If I really wanted to splurge, I'd get a bottle of one of their fancy shampoos.

The gift that Kevin had chosen for his girlfriend must've cost him a small fortune. He explained that he'd picked out all the items himself. I thought that Caroline was a lucky girl, indeed.

"Oh Kevin, she'll love it," I gushed, and I meant it. I handed the basket back to him. "Any girl would go crazy over that gift." And I couldn't help but feel just a tiny bit of envy for someone I had never even met.

Know Before You Go

Three Simple Rules for Backpacking on the Cheap:

1) Crash at someone else's place whenever you can.
It's amazing how much money you can save simply by pulling up some floor or couch at a family member's or friend's house. Plan your itinerary so that at least some of the destinations on it are within easy reach of people you know.

2) Stay in hostels
Once you've run out of family and friends to stay with, book yourself into youth hostels. If your student days are way behind you, take advantage of Elderhostels. Sure, you have to sleep in dormitory-style rooms and perform chores, and the management usually kicks you out from about 10am until 5pm or so, but you're there to go sightseeing anyway. You won't be spending much time in bed.

3) Eat only one big meal a day. You can snack for the other two.

✧ Chapter Twelve ✧

From mid-December, when classes broke up for the Christmas holiday, until mid-January, Kathy and I followed the Three Simple Rules almost religiously. For the first part of my travels, I rode Rule 1 for all it was worth. From December 17th until the 20th, I moved all my stuff out of Keynes College and installed myself at Colin's room in his Parkwood flat. The campus was almost entirely deserted, so I took advantage of the mostly empty laundry rooms (a rare occurrence) to make sure I had a stockpile of clean clothes. There would be no hand-washing undies in bathroom sinks for me!

On the 20th, I headed into London and stayed with my friend Robin. She had graduated from Mount Holyoke a few years ahead of me, and, like me, had spent her junior year abroad in England. She was now back doing a work abroad program. Robin lived in a bedsit; her private space consisted of a room that was both her bedroom and her living space. She shared a bathroom and kitchen with the other people on her floor.

Robin's bedsit was not a Herne Bay horror – it was in a beautiful Georgian townhouse that had once been a palatial single-family dwelling. So her bedroom/living room was actually well-appointed by bedsit standards, with high carved ceilings, hardwood floors, crown molding, a gas fireplace, and huge bay windows. And since it was up on the fourth floor, there was very little traffic noise from the streets below.

We had a great time hanging out and doing a little sightseeing (the Tate Gallery) and shopping (along Oxford Street, decorated for Christmas with garlands and giant ornaments that were strung overhead). I didn't dare buy a lot, since I was backpacking. Whatever I bought over the next three weeks or so I'd have to cart around in my backpack or pay to mail back to Canterbury. Neither option was terribly appealing. On the 22nd I left Robin and caught a train out to Epsom, where I'd spend the next week with Rosalind and her family. I was especially excited about this; we hadn't seen each other in a few years and had so much to catch up on. My mom was relieved that I'd be spending Christmas with a family, and a Catholic one at that. She'd been worried that I might be alone for the holidays, or even worse, not in church on Christmas Day.

I figured that since I'd breezed through Thanksgiving away from my family, Christmas away would be no problem, either. I couldn't have been more wrong. At least when I was at UKC over Thanksgiving, I'd been with all of my American friends, and we'd been preoccupied with the cooking. But as Christmas Eve approached, it hit me how far away I was from home and all of the traditions that I knew.

Christmas Eve was always my favorite part of the family holiday — even more so than Christmas Day. My mom cooked shrimp scampi for dinner, and we'd be joined by my Nina and Grampa, my mom's parents. Mom's "Music Box Christmas" album would be playing all night in the background. My dad would build a fire and Grampa would pass out glasses filled with Frangelico or Galliano. My best friend Kim would usually drop in at some point in the evening, and then we'd all head out to Midnight Mass.

Christmas Eve in England, however, was an entirely different scene. There was no special dinner. Instead, Rosalind and I ate a quick meal and headed down to the pubs with all of her friends. That was it. I was shocked – partying and drinking on what I considered one of the most peaceful, sacred nights of the year seemed like a sacrilege. I was terribly homesick and was beginning to wish I'd flown home for the Christmas break.

The only bright part of Christmas Eve had been a quick phone call with Sal; he happened to ring as Rosalind and I were getting ready to go out. When I heard his voice, I tried really hard to sound upbeat, but he could tell I was sad.

"Guess what?" he asked. "I've got a surprise for you. I got my passport photos done last week."

Since I'd arrived in England, Sal had hesitantly mentioned a few times that he might come to visit, if it was all right with me and if it fit into my schedule. But his job was demanding and he didn't have a lot of vacation time. I don't think either of us thought it would ever really happen.

I wasn't even sure he'd actually had the passport photos done; he was probably saying it to make me feel better because he knew this was my first Christmas away from home. I honestly didn't give it much serious thought at the time.

"Come on!" Rosalind urged. "Everybody's waiting for us down the pub." I'd ended the phone call quickly, and that would be the last opportunity I'd have to speak with Sal for the next three weeks or so.

When we finally got back to Rosalind's house after last call at the pubs, there was another surprise waiting. Unbeknownst to me, my mom had mailed my Christmas stocking to Rosalind's parents, along with my presents. I'd had this stocking since I was just a baby. My mom had made one for me, my sisters, herself, and my dad. When I saw mine in Rosalind's living room, I started to cry. I missed home so much at that moment that I vowed I'd never spend another Christmas away from my family.

December 28th saw me boarding another train, this time one that was bound for Coventry, where I'd crash at Arvine's through New Year's. Kathy was already up there, having spent Christmas with Arvine and her family. It was so great to see familiar faces again, and it was fun to meet Arvine's three brothers and her mum and dad.

I'd never been to the Midlands, as Arvine's part of England was called, and Kathy and I did a lot of exploring in the city. Coventry was bombed to bits during World War II and now consists almost entirely of new buildings, so it's not the place to go if you want to see authentic half-timbered houses and thatched roofs.

The city's beautiful old cathedral was, sadly, not spared from the war's destruction, and took a direct hit from a German bomb. The only thing left was the shell, but the city left it standing and linked it directly to the modern, new cathedral that went up right beside it. It was very thoughtfully and imaginatively executed, and even though I hated modern architecture, I had to admit it was very clever.

*The old and the new
side by side in Coventry.*

On a decidedly more secular note, Kathy and I also learned that Coventry was famous (or infamous) for Lady Godiva and her X-rated horseback ride through the city streets in her birthday suit. See – who says history can't be fun?!

On January 2nd, 1987, after ringing in the New Year with Arvine and her friends, Kathy and I began our Excellent Backpacking Adventure. For the next two weeks, we mainly stayed in hostels and subsisted almost completely on muesli, satsumas, baked beans, and jacket potatoes. It's a miracle that we didn't get sick with a serious vitamin deficiency, but we weren't about to waste our precious travel money on things as trivial as three square meals a day.

Say what?

Brit/Yank Translator

Muesli: *a granola-like cereal*
Satsumas: *clementine-sized oranges*
Jacket potatoes: *a baked potato that's slit open and topped with baked beans, prawns, cole slaw, or cheese*
Prawns: *small, bite-sized shrimp*

We began in Carlisle, where there was a lot to see in the city itself, including its castle and cathedral. For some reason that neither Kathy nor I was able to remember later, we never did make it to Hadrian's Wall – which was the reason we'd planned to go to Carlisle in the first place. The hostel was great, and we met a ton of people who were our age, so we had lots of company on the nightly walks to and from the pub that was just down the road.

Edinburgh and Glasgow were next; Edinburgh was our favorite of the two because it was so beautiful and walkable. It was also where I made my first splurge – an authentic Scottish kilt in the Lindsay tartan. It weighed a ton, but I'd wanted one for a long time; I had purposely left extra room in Colin's backpack for it. We'd picked clean, centrally located hostels in both cities, and aside from a couple of weirdos in the Glasgow hostel, the people we met were friendly.

First thing in the morning on January 7th, Kathy and I caught the ferry from Stranraer, Scotland to Larne, Northern Ireland. That night, we would be taking a break from Simple Rule #2; we were allowing ourselves a night in a bed and breakfast, one that was well recommended according to our *Let's Go*. It would be a wonderful treat to sleep in a comfy bed, sink our toes into proper wall-to-wall carpeting, and have the luxury of a private bathroom. The prospect of a traditional Irish breakfast the following morning was exciting, too.

Our *Let's Go* had said that although Larne was the gateway to Belfast, it did have a ruin in it called "Olderfleet Castle." The very name sounded romantic. We spent a while on the street in front of our B+B poring over our maps to figure out where it was, with no success. Larne was tiny, so there weren't exactly a lot of places for a castle to hide.

We finally gave up and asked two policemen who were nearby in their parked patrol car if they knew where

Olderfleet was. They started cracking up, which we thought was a little strange – we couldn't figure out what was so funny about a castle.

"Get in and we'll give you a lift," they said, so Kathy and I climbed into the back of their squad car. A minute or two later, we had arrived. "We'll just wait here for you girls. You'll be done in a minute," they added with another laugh as we got out.

Then we saw it: a pile of rocks that was once part of a tower belonging to a much larger, no longer existent castle. It had a small sign bolted to it that read "Olderfleet Castle." So much for our romantic Irish ruin. But it did make for an entertaining ride back to our B+B with the cops and a fun beginning for a postcard home. *"Dear Mom and Dad: we weren't in Northern Ireland for two hours before we were picked up by the police..."*

Olderfleet Castle.
Yep – that's it.

A coach ride from Larne into Belfast was next. As our coach pulled into the station, a soldier armed with a machine gun climbed on, walked all the way to the back of the coach, turned around, and came back down the aisle, giving everyone on the bus the hairy eyeball before he got off. Kathy and I were terrified and had visions of being casualties in an IRA bombing, which were all too common at the time.

As we walked around the city doing some sightseeing, we noticed there was something strange about the post boxes on the streets and in the walls. Instead of having nice wide slots for the mail like the ones in England and Scotland did, the post boxes in Northern Ireland had tiny little slits that were barely big enough to accommodate a thin envelope. We couldn't figure out why at first, but then we understood; a favorite calling card of the IRA was the letter bomb. It was sobering. We already knew we had so much to be thankful for in America, but here in Northern Ireland were more harsh reminders of just how insulated our native land was from terrorism.

The afternoon of January 8th found us on yet another train; we were going to Dublin, where we planned to visit Trinity College (The Book of Kells), St. Patrick's Cathedral (Jonathan Swift), and the Guinness Brewery (free samples of beer!), among other places. We'd already made a reservation at a small youth hostel and were looking forward to exploring a new city.

What we didn't realize at the time was that this "hostel" was an independent one. In other words, it wasn't part of the International Youth Hostel Association, which guaranteed certain amenities (like running water and central heat). After schlepping for what seemed like miles from the train station, we finally arrived at the place. The sun was already low in the sky, our backs were aching, and we were sweating like pigs under our winter coats. We were dying for a hot shower and a change of clothes.

From the moment we arrived, though, we got a bad feeling that steadily grew worse. For starters, we noticed that the neighborhood was one step above Skid Row and that the hostel smelled funny inside. What's more, the bathroom floor was filthy and littered with wet newspapers. Dust bunnies covered the dormitory floor. The kitchen looked as if it wouldn't pass a Board of Health inspection, and we could actually see our breath in it. Kathy and I had seen enough. We explained that we wouldn't be staying the night after all.

"What's not to your satisfaction?" the proprietor asked us. "What's wrong?"

I resisted the urge to give the smart-ass answer, "Oh, everything." Instead, we quietly said something about changing our minds, shouldered our packs, and began to plod all the way back to the center of Dublin, where we would have to look for the Tourist Information Bureau. It was now almost dark. I still hadn't gotten used to how far north the U.K. was; now that it was wintertime, the sun was setting by 3:30pm and it was usually dark by 4pm.

We had no place to stay, night was approaching, and everywhere we passed on the way back from the yukky "hostel" looked equally sleazy. We'd even been approached by a couple of shifty-looking guys on our way to the Tourist Information Bureau. We couldn't tell if they were harmless panhandlers or worse, and we didn't stick around long enough to find out.

At this point, Simple Rule #2 went right out the window and common sense took hold. Hostels in this part of Dublin were not looking like a wise option. We asked the man at the Tourist Information Bureau for a decent B+B in a safe area. He found us an adorable little place within a few minutes' walk of Trinity College that was run by an older man and woman who treated us like family.

When we told our hosts about our misadventures that afternoon, they sadly shook their heads and informed us that Dublin was in the grip of terrible unemployment, particularly among young people. Even worse, there was a heroin trafficking problem in certain areas of the city (probably where we'd just come from). It was a shame that we'd had such a bad introduction.

My brief journal entry that night said it all, really. I wrote: *Dublin sucks. I hope we make it out of here in one piece and still possessing certain things, like our wallets and our virginity.*

✧ Chapter Thirteen ✧

Despite the rough start, Dublin grew on us. Our first destination was Trinity College – specifically The Long Room in the library, where The Book of Kells and other illuminated manuscripts were housed. It was a thrill to see them up close. Trinity's campus was pretty, with buildings that were much older and more attractive than UKC's, but Kathy and I were still glad we hadn't decided to come here for our junior year abroad.

We saw the imposing St. Patrick's Cathedral, where Jonathan Swift, author of *Gulliver's Travels*, was the dean. And we stumbled upon a little gem of a church across the River Liffey called St. Michan's. Its claim to fame? Mummies. Seriously. Apparently the high lime content in the earth where the burial vaults are located was perfect for preserving bodies. There were several bodies on display behind plexiglass windows. Very macabre, but pretty cool all the same.

The vendors and shops along famous Grafton Street were interesting, and we both picked up a couple of small souvenirs for ourselves. We decided to bag the tour of the Guinness Brewery – it looked like it was in a dicey area. Instead, we visited St. Stephen's Green in Phoenix Park. It reminded us of a smaller version of London's Hyde Park.

Soon, though, it was time for our next stops: Cork and Blarney. On January 10th, we caught a train out of Dublin and after about a three-hour ride, we arrived in Cork just as it started to snow lightly. The snow would continue off and on for the rest of our stay in Ireland. The hostel in Cork was great, and in the living room we met Peter and Vicky, a young Australian couple who were backpacking through Ireland. They had a

rental car and offered to take us to Blarney with them
the next day.

Kathy and I agreed that it was much easier to meet people
in hostels than it was in B+Bs. Although the accommodations in
B+Bs are definitely more luxurious, the whole communal nature
of hostels encourages people to start chatting with each other
while they're cooking their evening meals, standing in line for
the shower, or getting ready for bed. You start making small talk
and before you know it, you've found people who are going to
the same places you are – instant travelling companions!

We hung out with Peter and Vicky for the two days we
stayed in Cork and Blarney and were sorry to say goodbye to
them. They were headed out to the Ring of Kerry, and we were
going back to Dublin, where we'd catch a bus to the ferry port
in Dun Laoghaire. From there we'd take the evening ferry
across the sea, followed by the long, overnight train to London.

It was a non-stop party from the ferry port in Dun Laoghaire
all the way into London. We'd picked the night crossing
because we figured it'd be quiet and we might actually be
able to sleep. But the ferry and the train were packed with
screaming babies, partying backpackers, and chain-
smoking/beer-swilling students.

We didn't get a wink of sleep, but we did meet Luc, a fun
French Canadian guy from Quebec. Luc was a free spirit who
was drifting aimlessly around the U.K. for the month before
he went back to school. He was headed into London for a while
and had no plans, so we invited him to come with us to the
hostel we'd booked in Wellgarth Road.

Now, the original idea had been for Kathy and me to wind up our backpacking trip by spending a night or two in London. Then we'd take a fast train to Canterbury and arrive the day before classes started up again. But the weather had other plans for us. The light snow that had begun falling in Cork continued and got worse as our night ferry left Dun Laoghaire. By the time our overnight train pulled into London at 6am, the fast-moving snowstorm had dumped several inches on the city.

The capital looked beautiful, but London is not a city that's used to lots of snow. Five inches of the white stuff at home would've been nothing; the roads would've been plowed and clear in no time. But London's untreated, snowy streets were treacherous for cars and buses. The Tube was running, fortunately, and we'd planned to spend a night or two in the city anyway. So we enjoyed the wintry scenery and laughed about what Londoners would do if they had to endure a New England winter.

What we didn't realize was that the storm had already unleashed its full fury on Kent. Record-high snowfall (up to two feet in some parts) crippled the southeast, and gale-force winds created snowdrifts that reached up to the tops of the hedges along the roads. Trains were frozen to the tracks. The highways and secondary roads into Kent were completely impassable; entire towns and villages were cut off. Even the lorry drivers couldn't get through.

Say what?
Brit/Yank Translator

Lorry:
tractor-trailer truck

145

On the TV stations and in the newspapers, there was talk of the snowstorm being the worst one that Kent had seen in more than 40 years. From the warm sitting room in our London youth hostel, Kathy and I watched the evening news and groaned. There was no way we were going to be back on campus in two days for the start of classes.

But if you're going to get stranded somewhere for a few days, London is the perfect place for it to happen. Kathy and I quickly became experts at finding free and almost-free things to do in the city while we waited for Kent to re-open to the outside world. Many of London's museums, we discovered, had free admission; lots of the ones that did charge had reduced-fee days or offered the all-important student discount. All we had to do was plan our visits accordingly.

At the end of each day's sightseeing, we'd stop in at Victoria Station to see if the trains were running out to Kent yet. My journal entries for the London part of our backpacking trip all began the same way: *We are still stuck in London* or *We are still at the Wellgarth Road hostel* or *Still no trains out to Kent.* It wasn't as if it was a hardship. As long as we had clean underwear and enough cash to buy food and our train tickets back to campus, we were fine.

Finally, on our fourth day in London, we heard that train service to Kent had been restored at last. It didn't matter that we'd be late for the start of classes; most people were probably in the same boat (or dogsled) we were. Nevertheless, we were looking forward to seeing Julie, Bob, Arvine, and the rest of our friends. I was excited to tell Colin and Kevin about everything we'd seen and done. And I was really looking forward to not carrying everything I owned on my back.

On the train ride to Canterbury, Kathy and I talked excitedly about what we'd do first when we got back. We couldn't decide: dump our packs and go straight to The Dog and Bear with Arvine and the gang? Catch evensong at the cathedral? Hang at the Keynes bar? Set up camp in the dreaded laundry room? Skip the laundry and just burn all the clothes we'd worn to threads?

"Oh, I don't know," Kathy finally admitted. "It'll be awesome just to get home."

"I know," I agreed. "I can't wait."

Then we stopped and smiled at each other as we realized what we'd just said. We'd called Canterbury "home."

London for Free

Many first-time visitors to London make the erroneous assumption that the city is outrageously expensive; however, one of the nicest things about the capital is that so many of its attractions are 100% free. Visit **www.londonforfree.net** for an exhaustive list of ideas, locations, and times. Here are some suggestions to get you started:

Museums – Unless you visit a special exhibition, there is no admission fee at most of London's major museums and galleries. My personal favorites are The Victoria & Albert, The Museum of London, The Imperial War Museum, and Sir John Soane's Museum. You could easily fill an entire week in these places.

Street Markets – London is famous for its lively street markets. It costs nothing to stroll around and watch the vendors and shoppers haggle with each other. Camden Market, Portobello Road Market, and Borough Market are the most exciting and colorful ones, but there are lots of smaller ones as well.

Parks – London's parks and gardens are an amazing treasure. By all means, treat yourself to a relaxing (and free) visit to the biggies like Hyde Park and Green Park. But don't miss Postman's Park, a wonderful little surprise that is bordered by King Edward Street, Little Britain, and Aldersgate Street.

Lunchtime concerts – Many of London's smaller churches (and some of the big ones) put on free organ or choral concerts that are open to the public.

Part Two

Back at UKC, life quickly returned to normal and things picked up almost exactly where they'd left off before the Christmas break. Except for poor Kevin. I'd gone to visit him in C Block shortly after I'd moved all my things out of Colin's Parkwood flat and back into my room at Keynes.

"So, how was your Christmas?" I asked him as we gave each other a big hug.

"Awful. Caroline finished with me. On Christmas, of all the bloody days she could've picked."

"Oh, Kevin, I'm so sorry." I wanted to punch Caroline for dumping somebody as sweet and thoughtful as Kevin. In an instant, I'd gone from being slightly envious of her to hating her guts. I was a little surprised at how strongly I felt.

"Never mind. It's done."

"Well, that definitely warrants a pint at the Keynes bar. Come on — I'm buying."

A couple of weeks after classes started up again, Kathy and I had already made travel plans for the month-long Easter break that would be coming up at the beginning of April. This time we'd be going to Europe for part of it — we'd decided to book a one-week coach tour to Italy, where we'd "do" Rome, Florence, Venice, Pisa, and Orvieto. We'd be joined by Julie and one of her UC San Diego friends, a girl named Sharolyn, whom we'd gotten to know before the Christmas break.

The remaining part of Easter break was filling up quickly, too. Once we returned from our Italian tour, I was going to travel down to Bath (Jane Austen country) and Glastonbury (huge destination for Arthurian legend fans). After that, Jon, my royal family-hating, ballroom dancing buddy from up north, was having me to stay with his family for a few days. He was going to show me around York – and, as a special treat, we were going to visit the Bronte Parsonage. Since we were both English majors, this was a big deal. That pretty much left only Easter weekend unplanned. Nobody had come up with any ideas for that yet, but there was still plenty of time to sort things out.

It was around the time that we were making all these plans that I phoned Sal. It had been a while since we'd spoken. Our once weekly phone calls had tapered off to every couple of weeks or so. I had gotten so busy with my friends, the rowing club, the ballroom dancing club, and my classes (in that order) that I just didn't have the time to write and call Sal as frequently or regularly as I had done during my first term.

Sal, however, had continued to write me long, flowery letters that I still received as often as once and sometimes even twice a week. It had gotten to the point where I didn't even need to read his letters all that carefully anymore. Each one pretty much said the same thing: *I miss you, I love you, I wonder what you're doing right now, I wonder when I'll see you again, blah blah blah blah blah.* There might be some news about work, but for the most part the letters were predictable. I felt a little guilty that he wasn't hearing from me as regularly as I was hearing from him.

During this particular phone call, I'd just told him in great detail about all of my plans for the Easter break. He'd listened quietly to the excitement in my voice. Then there was silence on the other end of the line before he asked, "So do you have any plans for the Easter weekend yet?"

"Huh? Easter? No – we haven't planned that far ahead. I'm sure we'll think of something." I started rattling off the names of all the places in England that I still wanted to see before the end of the school year when Sal suddenly interrupted me.

"Diane, I'm asking because I'd like to come out for Easter weekend – if it's all right with you. I don't want to wreck any plans you might be making with your friends."

"Oh wow! You're serious. You really want to fly out." This announcement had come as a complete surprise. So he'd been telling the truth about getting his passport photos after all. I was caught off guard and was at a loss for words (something that did not happen very often with me).

"That wasn't exactly the reaction I was hoping for."

"No, no, Sal. I'm just surprised. I didn't think you had the vacation time. Of course I'd like to see you. Easter weekend is wide open. It's just an awful lot of money to spend for such a short visit."

"Let me worry about that. So I can go ahead and book my flight?"

"Yes, sure. Just let me know the details and I can plan some things for us to do."

"Diane, I can't wait to see you."

"Same here. Bye for now."

So Sal was really coming to England after all these months. How did I feel? To be honest, kind of weird. We hadn't seen each other since last October, and we hadn't dated all that long before I left for England – just a few months. I had no real rea-

153

son to say no that I could think of. I wasn't involved with any-body here in England, although many of my friends were guys. I wondered if it would be awkward introducing him to them.

This would be Sal's first trip outside the U.S., so now I also had the pressure of planning something memorable. Was I ready for that responsibility? And what would he be expecting from me? Surely he didn't think that everything would be the same as before? I was already a different person from the one who'd said goodbye to him at Logan Airport.

I should've said no to the visit when he'd first told me he'd had his passport photos taken. I could've stopped everything right then and there. But my stupid sense of politeness and a large amount of guilt had taken over. Here I was in England having this terrific year, with one new experience after another.

And there he was stuck back in America in the same old job and counting the days until I came home. I guess I felt like I somehow owed it to him to let him come over and visit. And, I reminded myself, neither of us had made any promises to the other. The visit would be exactly what we decided to make it. So why did I have such a knot in my stomach about it?

Kevin's birthday on February 3rd was a welcome distraction from my worries about having to plan the Perfect Weekend. The birthday boy had hired a minibus to take a bunch of us to Nero's Discotheque in nearby Ramsgate. We all had a fun night of dancing and never got back until the early hours of the next morning. I worried that with Valentine's Day coming, Kevin might still be a little sad about Caroline breaking up with him.

So I thought I'd surprise him with a cute Valentine's Day card.

I happened to mention it to Colin one night over dinner, and he said, "Oh, you mustn't sign your name – you'll spoil the fun."

"What do you mean? How's Kevin going to know it's from me if I don't sign my name?"

"That's exactly the point. Over here, you're supposed to guess who your Valentine is from the hints they leave on the card."

Hints? Here was an opportunity to get creative and make Kevin laugh at the same time. I sat down to compose a little rhyme and got carried away (typical English major). I was quite proud of the results. It read:

Roses are red, violets are blue.
Your first name is Kevin, your last name is Clue!

Hope you're reading this card by the dawn's early light,
trying to guess my identity with all of your might.

I'll give you some hints, but only a few.
The windows of my soul are the color of blue.

You're wracking your brain. Here is a giant pause...
Has anyone ever told you you're a rebel without a cause?

The time draws nigh that I must depart.
I've given you four, now here is my heart.

I hand-drew a little heart at the bottom with a "?" underneath and checked the four clues I'd worked into the poem: I'd used the American term "last name" instead of the English term "surname"; I'd quoted a small section of "The Star-Spangled Banner"; I'd revealed my eye color; and I'd included the titles of my favorite James Dean movies. At the very least, Kevin would figure out that an American was behind the Valentine. I put the poem away in my top desk drawer and decided that I would pin it to the Student Urgent Notice Board right after breakfast on Valentine's Day.

Not long after Kevin's birthday was Kathy's 21st, so there was another excuse to go out and celebrate. Aedan, one of the Americans from the USC contingent, had ordered a massive cake as a special surprise for Kathy's big birthday. It was big enough to feed everyone with leftovers to spare. I got a hilarious photo of Kathy leaning out her bedroom window holding the cake and looking up at me while I leaned out of my bedroom window and looked down to take the picture. One slip from Kathy and those Keynes ducks would've had the most decadent snack they'd ever eaten.

Two other milestones took place during February, and they both happened on Valentine's Day. The rowing club made its first appearance at the Henley Heads event. It was an early, Saturday-morning wakeup call and a long drive out from Canterbury to Henley, but the day was an absolute blast. Amatsia drove the club's van, which also towed the trailers loaded with the boats. We all sat in the back of the van and Amatsia cranked the soundtrack to "The Big Chill" on the tape deck. It had become our official road music and we always listened to it on the way to and from practice each week.

We didn't do half-bad, considering it was our first race. There was no winner's trophy for the *Kentish Hops*, but I was secretly glad – it was freezing cold that day, and the tradition for a winning boat is for the crew to throw its cox into the river. That was an honor I could happily do without.

The Kentish Hops takes on the Henley Heads.

After the obligatory pint at a pub in Henley, we had just enough time to stash the boats at the boathouse, rush back to UKC, and shower. That night was the annual Rag Ball – not quite as posh as the UNA Ball, since there was no sit-down dinner. But it was a much-anticipated night all the same. All of our other friends were already at Eliot waiting for us, so Ian and I walked over together from Keynes.

By the time we arrived at the Eliot dining hall, the party was in full swing. We quickly found Kathy, Jon, Kevin, and a bunch of other people from the ballroom dancing club. Everybody wanted to know how we'd done at the Henley Heads, so Ian and I filled them in.

"Diane brought honor to UKC with her large American mouth!" Ian said as he clapped me on the back and put his arm around my shoulders. "That's a direct quote from Amatsia."
I *had* been pretty loud; in fact Amatsia told me after the race that one of the coaches standing beside him on the riverbank remarked that I was the loudest cox he'd ever heard. And I now had the hoarse voice to prove it.

"Well, I had a ton of help," I said as I threw my arms around Ian's waist. "Especially from the A Crew's stroke."

"Oh stop, you'll make me blush." Ian pretended to be embarrassed.

"You're both going to make me throw up," Kathy said. "Let's dance."

Of course, just as the music was really getting good, the DJ had to go and play a slow song. Danny, one of my buddies from the ballroom dancing club, appeared beside me.

"Don't forget that you promised me the first slow number,

my love." He gave me a mock bow and a silly grin.

"Of course – I'd never forget you," I answered, as we started to dance.

At the end of the song, Danny excused himself and blew me a kiss. "I must go and bring joy to the rest of the ladies in the room."

"O.K., you go do that. I don't think I could've handled the excitement of two dances in a row with you, anyway." I was still giggling as I started to walk toward the edge of the dance floor where my friends were waiting. There was a sudden tap on my back, and I turned around to see Kevin.

"Why did you run off with Danny like that? I was just getting ready to ask you to dance."

"Oh, I'm sorry – I didn't realize you were waiting. Hey, you're in luck. Listen – the DJ's playing another slow one."

We walked back into the center of the floor. The song that had just started, Roxy Music's cover of the John Lennon hit "Jealous Guy," had become one of my favorites over the last few months. Out of habit, Kevin and I automatically assumed the ballroom dancing "ready position" and then laughed at ourselves.

"Hmmm – is 'Jealous Guy' a rumba in your opinion, or is it more of a bossanova?" I asked.

"Neither. I think it's just a good old-fashioned slow dancing song." Kevin slid both arms around my waist and I put mine up around his neck. Babs was right; Kevin was exactly one head taller than me. I suppose it did make a nice-looking silhouette.

"So, your first race was a success?" he asked as we swayed back and forth.

"Well, we didn't win any medals or anything, but we didn't embarrass ourselves, either. And I didn't sink our boat or anyone else's. So yes – I think that qualifies as a success."

"Well done." Kevin pulled me really close and gave me a long hug. I rested my head on his shoulder; he smelled good. Why hadn't I ever noticed that before? I looked up to tell him something else about the race and he was looking down at me with a strange expression on his face. Before I knew it, he had leaned down and kissed me. It was the softest, most gentle kiss a guy had ever given me. I hadn't seen it coming. My head was swimming. Then Kevin kissed me again. After a little while he pulled away, and then I felt his lips barely brush my ear.

"I'm not sure that should've happened," he whispered.

"Well, I liked it," I admitted, stunned at what I'd just said.

"I liked it as well. Happy Valentine's Day, Diane. And thank you for the lovely poem."

"You guessed! Were the hints that easy?"

"Yes – besides, only you would've written an epic poem instead of a simple hint."

Chapter Fifteen

"He did *what*?!" Julie shrieked. "What did you do?"

"I kissed him back, of course!"

We were sitting in Julie's room, where I had run as soon as I'd gotten up the next morning. Judging from Julie's reaction, Kathy hadn't told her the big news.

"Well...what was it like?"

"It was – oh wow – I mean – how do you describe something like that? I had no idea he was going to do it. I mean, I'm glad he did it, and it was amazing, but, oh – this just makes everything so *confusing*!"

"It's not confusing at all. He likes you."

"I like him, too. Very much. We're such good friends. But last night changes everything!"

"How does it change everything? It was just a kiss. You're overthinking it."

"You don't just walk up to someone and kiss them. He has lots of friends who are girls, but I don't see him kissing *them*. I don't want to be Rebound Girl. Caroline broke up with him not even two months ago. And Sal's coming over to visit in April. What do I do? Oh, this is such a mess!"

"Yeah, O.K., a real mess. Two guys after you. I wish I had your problems. Why don't you just talk to Kevin and ask him how he feels?"

"Then he'll think I'm some crazy person who's all obsessed with why he kissed me."

"But you kind of *are*."

"Julie, you're not helping. Tell me what I should do."

"You really never saw this coming? Diane, everyone saw

this coming – except you. We just can't believe it didn't happen sooner. You spend all kinds of time together. He's a great guy."

"I knooooow."

"Now you're whining."

"Stop making fun of me! I feel like I've cheated on Sal."

"Oh my God. It's not like you slept with Kevin. Didn't you and Sal agree to see how this year went and not make any promises to each other?"

"Well...yes. But he's coming over in April, for God's sake. He's already bought his ticket."

"So? You'll have a great visit and then he'll go home. I'm sure he doesn't think you've been living like a nun over here."

"You make it sound like I'm some kind of slut."

"O.K., we all know *that* couldn't be farther from the truth. You want my opinion? I think you're basically a nice person and you didn't want to hurt Sal's feelings. So when he asked if he could come visit you in England you said yes. It's a visit – it's not like you're agreeing to marry him."

"I guess you're right. But it probably would've made things easier if I'd told him he couldn't come out in the first place."

"Maybe. But when he asked what your plans were for Easter weekend, none of this had happened with Kevin yet. So you had no reason to say no to Sal. Go talk to Kevin. I think you'll feel better."

Before ballroom dancing club that Monday, I went over to C Block and knocked on Kevin's door. Luckily, when he opened it, he was there on his own.

"Oh hello, Diane. Did you want to walk over to ballroom dancing together? You're a bit early. Care for a cup of tea?"

"No thanks. Kevin, I was actually wondering if we could talk before we go over to Eliot."

"Sure – what did you want to talk about?"

Honestly, guys could be really thick sometimes. Did I have to spell it out for him? "Well, I was wondering why you kissed me on Saturday night at the Rag Ball."

"Why did I kiss you? Why did you think I kissed you? What kind of a question is that?" I couldn't tell if he was hurt or angry, or both. Regardless, I'd really screwed things up now. I never should've listened to Julie.

"Well, it's just that since Saturday night, I've been thinking a lot about what happened. It's kind of a big deal. Don't you think?"

"Yes."

"I really like you, Kevin. A lot."

"And I like you a lot. That's why I bloody kissed you."

"So, what do we do now? I mean, I don't want you to think I'm getting all weird on you, but this kind of changes things between us. At least I think so."

"I'm sorry if I upset you. I certainly didn't mean to do that."

"No, you haven't. It's just that I'm confused. You're one of my best friends here, but now I think I want to be more than friends. And I guess I wasn't sure if you felt the same way – until Saturday, anyway. I'll be going back to America in June or July. So it's not like we have all kinds of time if we do start going out. But if we really like each other, should that matter? I don't know…I'm not making sense, am I?"

"Diane, do you think I haven't thought about all of this already? I really, *really* wanted to kiss you – way before the Rag Ball. But you have somebody back in America. And honestly, I'm afraid that if we do start 'going out,' as you call it, it's going to change how you feel about Sal. Maybe you'll start finding fault with him. Or with me."

"Shouldn't I be the one who decides that for myself?"

"I think that we should be practical. There's only half of Lent term left, and then the Easter break. We won't even see each other during the break because you'll be traveling. Once we come back, there's just Trinity term. Then it's goodbye."

Now I was getting angry. "Well, maybe you should've thought about that before you kissed me. What did you think was going to happen?"

"This! This is exactly what I was afraid would happen, Diane. What if we start something and then after a while we decide that we're better off being friends after all? Then our friendship is ruined."

"Oh, O.K. – so for the next three or four months our friendship is going to be strained, because we both know that we'd really like more but we're not going to do anything about it. That's great."

"Diane, all I can tell you right now is that I don't think it'll work out with us being a couple."

"So that's it? You're not even going to think about it?"

"Look, I'm confused too. I promise you I'll think about things, and we can have another talk."

"Well, I hope it's soon, because I hate waiting, and I hate

not knowing what's going on. I really like you, Kevin. There, at least we know how I feel about things. We'd better leave for Eliot, or we're going to be late."

Ballroom dancing was going to be really awkward tonight. All I wanted to do was get through it, go back to my room, and cry.

✦ Chapter Sixteen ✦

A week or so later, Kevin and I talked about "us" (or the lack thereof) and we reluctantly came to the conclusion that the only sensible and practical thing to do was to remain friends. If we never started going out, then we wouldn't have to worry about wrecking our friendship and facing a mess in the summer when it was time for me to return to the States. Things would be easier that way, especially with Sal's visit looming. It sucked, but it was the least complicated way to handle the situation.

I was glad I had something else to occupy my time after that conversation; the rowing club was going to compete in the Medway Heads in Maidstone, Kent in a few days. All of us on the A Crew had been putting in lots of practice time. Amatsia thought that we might actually have a shot at placing in the top ten this time around, so we were really excited. We were even going to have a small cheering section in Maidstone, because a few of our friends had decided to come along and stand on the towpath at the midpoint.

The day of the race we were all in high spirits. It started off well enough; thanks to Ian's ambitious pace-setting, we were flying along at a good clip. There were a ton of boats entered, and the river was packed with them. Between yelling out commands, watching for other boats, and keeping an eye on everybody's form in the *Kentish Hops*, I was pretty busy.

About halfway through the course, though, I began to worry that we'd gone out too fast. If Ian and I weren't careful, there'd be nothing left to draw on for a sprint at the end of the race.

"What do you think?" Ian asked while he made seemingly effortless pulls on his blade. "How do we look?"

I quickly scanned everyone else's blades; they were all
moving in perfect time to Ian's stroke, but Dennis and William
were really straining with each pull. Gordon was looking a little
tired, too. We couldn't keep up this pace for the rest of the
course. "I think we need to take it easy for a little while,"
I answered.

"Fair enough. Call it, then."

The slightly slower pace seemed to be just what everybody
needed to catch their breath. As we neared the final portion of
the course, I felt like it was time to call for more steam. "Come
on, UKC," I screamed. "I want this boat going so fast that I get
bruises on my back. NEXT STROKE, FULL CREW, FULL
PRESSURE, ARE YOU READY...GO!"

At my command, the *Kentish Hops* took off like a bat out
of hell. With each pull of the blades, the small of my back
slammed against the edge of my hard, wooden cox's seat;
tomorrow I'd definitely have those black-and-blue marks
I'd just asked for.

There were shouts from the towpath on the riverbank as we
sped along the course, but all I heard was my own voice and
the grunts of the guys as they gave the last stretch of the race
everything they had. We were on fire, and it felt awesome.
As we rounded the final corner and began the sprint for the
finish line, I let myself imagine our boat's name at the top of
the standings.

Then disaster struck. To my horror, William caught a crab —
every rower's worst nightmare. His oar went into the river and

suddenly jerked as if an unseen person beneath the water had yanked it with great force. The blade slammed into William's midsection and nearly knocked him out of his seat. He lost his grip on the handle as it popped out of its gate. Only a split-second reaction saved the blade (and him along with it) from flying into the river.

William frantically tried to fit the blade back into its gate. In the meantime, I screamed, "HOLD IT UP!" We were now dead in the water; all we could do was watch helplessly as boat after boat flashed by us and capitalized on our incredibly bad luck. We could forget about a top-ten finish now.

"William, how's that blade?" I shouted as calmly as I could while he struggled. Inside I was panicking. I felt like I was going to throw up. Ian, staring at me, sat quietly, but his face was as white as a sheet. "He's nearly there, Ian," I said softly. "Any second now."

"Ready!" William bellowed from his seat. He was red-faced, furious, and soaked in sweat.

"All right, guys," I hollered. More boats streaked past us. "NEXT STROKE, FULL CREW, FULL PRESSURE, ARE YOU READY...GO!"

What should've been a glorious finale was a totally demoralizing limp across the finish line. Worse still, the whole thing had happened so close to the end and after such a promising start. Ours was one of the last boats to finish, so the noise from the spectators had pretty much died down. All along the river, it was quiet.

The silence was shattered suddenly by William's angry

scream of "FUCK!" It echoed off the riverbanks and bounced up and down the river. If he had yelled it five minutes earlier, nobody would've heard him in all the commotion of the race. But now, all eyes were upon us as every single person within earshot turned to stare openmouthed at the uncouth morons in the *Kentish Hops*.

I was mortified. If I could've stood up without capsizing the lot of us, I would have. I was that upset. I drew myself up in my seat as tall as I could while still sitting, and I glared down the boat straight at William. "THERE WILL BE NO "F" WORDS IN MY BOAT!" I screeched at the top of my lungs. Then I stopped. I couldn't think of anything else to add.

"Ah, that's capital, William," Ian said with deadpan delivery. "Excellent. Here we all sit with 'Kent University' emblazoned on our backs. They all know who we are now."

It was a long, quiet ride back to Canterbury.

✦ Chapter Seventeen ✦

I don't remember doing a whole lot of studying during March; my journal entries for the month were full of detailed reports about rowing, ballroom dancing events, a City of London Sinfonia concert at The Marlowe Theater, plays at the university, and a night out at London's West End to see "Starlight Express," among other things. I'd become an even bigger procrastinator over here than I was at home, and that was saying something. Oh well – there was always Reading Week to catch up on all of the essays that were due before Easter break began.

Now, the theory of Reading Week is that you're supposed to use it to catch up on any loose ends you might have with your studies so that you're better prepared for the third and final term of the university year. The reality was that I'd been putting off most of my essays all term and now had a truly scary backlog of work that needed to be finished by the end of March.

But like I said, I had more pressing concerns – like my social life. One of the things that we'd really been looking forward to was the Dance to France. It was a fancy dress ball. I'd be going with Kevin, Jon, Ian, and the rest of the C Block crew, in addition to Arvine and Bob. It basically involved an all-night booze cruise from Dover, complete with DJ, on a specially chartered overnight ferry to Calais, France. And lest anyone think that it was a night of complete debauchery, it was a fundraiser for Save the Children.

For the two weeks leading up to the event, we'd been busily making our costumes with the able assistance of Jon — who was a better seamstress than any woman I'd ever met. I was going to be a mouse, and Jon had engineered an adorable pair of ears for me out of pink and black felt. He'd then sewn them onto a pair of old-fashioned, hinged hair clips. The ears were attached to the top half of the clip so that I could then slide the whole thing into my hair at the top of my head. I was in awe of Jon's creativity and his skill with needle and thread; I couldn't even sew a button onto a shirt, much to my mom's disappointment. All I could manage was braiding the yarn for my mouse-tail.

Kevin was going to be a rabbit, complete with an oversized cottontail made out of faux-shearling and stuffed with polyfill. He'd sewn it himself, of course, along with his floppy bunny ears. On the night of the Dance to France, we'd do our animal faces using the contents of my makeup bag – under Jon's art direction.

"What is it with you two?" I asked them one lazy Sunday morning as we were working away in Kevin's room. "You're both way more domestic than any girls I know. I'm starting to get a little scared. What are you going to do for your next act? Whip

171

up an eight-course dinner, maybe?"

"Well, we were planning to do a Sunday roast later today if you'd like to join us," Jon said. "As soon as we finish with these costumes, we're heading to Sainsbury's to do the shopping." Between him and Kevin, they had a collection of pots, pans, and cooking tools that I'd never seen them actually use, although I'd heard about their famous Sunday roasts. I'd finally been invited.

If you wanted to cook on campus and you didn't live in the Parkwood flats, you had to go grocery shopping at the last minute. That's because back in the mid '80s, we didn't have refrigerators in any of the four colleges or in our rooms – unless you counted what we all jokingly referred to as the "Keynes fridge." These were plastic shopping bags that you hung around the knob on the radiator under your study-bedroom's window and then suspended outside the window itself.

If you stood out in the quads at any of the colleges and looked up on any given day from winter until early spring, you'd see at least a dozen such bags. They worked pretty well, unless there was an unexpected thaw or a really sunny day, in which case you ate or drank the contents of the bag at your own risk.

I wondered what kind of magic Kevin and Jon were going to work with the two-burner hot plate and toaster oven in their corridor's kitchenette. It had been a long while since I'd eaten a home-cooked meal – Arvine's house back in January, to be precise. I wasn't about to pass up this opportunity, so I gave Jon a few pounds to cover my share of the groceries. And I promised to help with the washing up.

The guys prepared a roast beef with roasted potatoes, carrots, parsnips, peas, and real, homemade gravy – without lumps. There was an awful lot of pan-jockeying and burner-shuffling with the hot plate, but the secret weapon was an electric skillet that Jon produced from under his bed.

"Hey, my mom has one of those," I marveled as he piled the seasoned roast and oil-coated potatoes into it. "But she uses it for fried dough or Swedish meatballs." I was both impressed and embarrassed by how much more self-sufficient English students were than their American counterparts.

Dance to France day finally arrived on March 6th, and everyone was looking forward to the coming night. In the afternoon I brought my costume and makeup bag over to C Block so that I could get ready later with Kevin, Jon, and Ian. Then we all walked into Canterbury to make a few last-minute purchases at some of the shops. We were about to go into Boots when I noticed Laura, a girl we knew from the ballroom dancing club, walking towards us in a huge hurry. She looked worried.

"Doing a little shopping, I see?"

"We forgot the black eyeliner. We need it to draw our whiskers," I answered. That sounded weird. "For our Dance to France costumes."

"Oh dear – haven't you heard?"

"Heard what?"

"The Dance to France has been cancelled."

"What?!" We all said at once.

"Afraid so. There's been some kind of ferry accident or something. There were notes on all of the Porters' Urgent Notice Boards. Didn't you see them?"

We shook our heads; none of us had checked the Keynes board on the way out.

"So that's it? Do you know anything else?" Kevin asked Laura.

"Only that there's to be an assembly at 5pm in the Senate building. I reckon they'll tell us more then. I'm ever so glad I saw all of you."

As we filed into the Senate, we saw that several of the university's administration and faculty members were down front, and most of them were stone-faced. Some were talking with each other in low voices while they looked at us. The mood was somber. One of them – an administrator whom I didn't rec- ognize – approached the microphone and began to speak.

"I'm afraid I have some very bad news to share with all of you," he started. "A terrible tragedy has occurred. A British car and passenger ferry bound for England has capsized off the coast of Zeebrugge [Belgium] and there's been a great loss of life. The authorities have set up an emergency meeting point in Dover for the families of those who died in the accident."

A buzz went up from all of us gathered in the building. Many of us, especially the American students, had lost track of how many ferries we'd caught for day trips or weekend breaks on the continent. It could just as easily have been any of us on that doomed ferry.

The man at the podium cleared his throat into the microphone. "Please, everyone. Your attention – many thanks. Out of respect to the deceased and their grieving families, tonight's Dance to France chartered ferry out of Dover has been cancelled. We'll be rescheduling the event into May and will let you know as soon as we've selected a new date. If you'd prefer to have the cost of your original ticket reimbursed, please make yourself known to us as you leave the building. That's all."

Nearly 200 people lost their lives in the frigid waters of the English Channel in what came to be known as the Zeebrugge Ferry Disaster. It was one of Britain's worst peacetime disasters at sea. On that sad evening, lots of us called home simply to tell our parents that we loved them and were O.K.

Chapter Eighteen

By the time Easter break rolled around, I had managed (thanks to lots of caffeine, a few all-nighters, and a healthy dose of fear), to slog my way through all of my essays. True to form, I turned in the final essay at the last possible moment – why ruin a perfect record? It wasn't exactly a literary masterpiece, but it was done, and that's what mattered most.

It was weird and awkward saying goodbye to Kevin. "Have a lovely time in Italy," he said. "And I hope your visit with Sal is everything you want it to be." He looked a little sad and it seemed like he wanted to say more, but he didn't.

Our girls' trip to Italy was one of those whirlwind coach tours, like in the 1970s movie *If It's Tuesday This Must Be Belgium*. Since none of us spoke a word of Italian (Kathy and I spoke French, while Sharolyn and Julie spoke Spanish) we figured this was the safest way to go. Nobody wanted to plan the trip, either. With an organized tour, we'd get a pre-planned itinerary with all of Italy's "greatest hits" and an interpreter, to boot.

It was just seven days, but we managed to pack a lot into the week. We were completely exhausted by the end of it. Coach tours are definitely not for the faint of heart or for people who like to sleep late – we grew to hate the early morning calls where you had to have your suitcase packed and sitting outside your hotel room door at 6am.

That said, we got a wonderful overview of Italy and met some fantastic people, which is another benefit of a coach tour. We were the youngest people on the tour – just like when we went to ballroom dancing events. There was one group of older ladies on the tour that we especially loved. We nicknamed them

"The Katharine Hepburn Clan" because one of them was a dead-ringer for the actress. There were four of them and they were slim, glamorous, and worldly-looking, with stylish clothes, perfectly coiffed silver hair, and fabulous accessories.

"I hope we're like that when we're retired," I said to Julie. Aside from the obvious attractions of Italy, like its art, history, food, and culture, we were also quite taken with Italian men. Every single one we saw seemed to be more hunky than the last – and what a bunch of flirts they were! They had a wonderful way of making you feel like a supermodel, with their dazzling smiles and their admiring calls of "Bella! Bella!"

One of the most interesting things we saw on our Italian trip was the crypt of the Capuchin Friars in Rome, under the church of Santa Maria della Concezione dei Cappuccini. It was way off the beaten tourist track and took us a while to find. Sharolyn had heard about it from one of her German friends back at UKC who was planning to attend seminary.

The place was so remote, in fact, that we had a hard time finding it and almost missed its small front door on the via Vittorio Veneto. We had to ring the doorbell and wait for an ancient Italian Capuchin friar to answer and let us in. There were lots of smiles and a ton of sign language exchanged, but the place spoke for itself and needed no translation. It was just as well, because the signs and pamphlets inside were entirely in Italian.

The "crypt," which was actually a six-room affair, was decorated from top to bottom with the disassembled bones of more than 4,000 deceased Capuchin friars. Everything from the floor that we walked on (knuckles) to the chandeliers hanging from the ceiling (vertebrae and ribs) was made entirely of human bones. We'd never seen anything quite like it. Once we got over the initial jolt of shock of walking on dead people, it was actually pretty fascinating to see how artistically the bones were used and displayed.

In several locations, entire skeletons had been left intact wearing the Capuchins' brown hooded robes; we gathered from our guide's reverent looks at the skeletons that this was a huge honor.

The old friar who took us around seemed delighted to have four young, non-Italian visitors. He chattered away in lightning-fast Italian and gestured happily to this or that feature. I caught a few isolated words that sounded like their French counterparts, but mostly we acted impressed, nodded our heads a lot, and said "Si!" as enthusiastically as we could. It was a fascinating glimpse into something that a lot of tourists never see. Years later, when my mom and dad visited Italy for their first time, they made a special point of visiting the Capuchin crypt because they'd been so taken with my description of it.

Out of all the places we visited on our Italian tour – Rome, Orvieto, Florence, Pisa, Bologna, and Venice – my personal favorite was Florence. The Merchant Ivory film adaptation of E.M. Forster's *A Room with a View* had been released in England right before we left for Italy, and Kathy and I had eagerly gone to see it at the Canterbury cinema.

Once we arrived in Florence, I think we drove poor Julie and Sharolyn crazy with our frequent squeals of, "Oh look! Just like in *A Room with a View!*" We half-expected to see Julian Sands or Helena Bonham-Carter pop out from behind a fountain or statue. The city was gorgeous, just like in the movie, and I hated to leave.

Venice was probably our most eagerly anticipated stop on the tour. When I was a little girl, my Auntie Karen and Uncle Ed had visited it on their honeymoon. I loved hearing their stories about the city; it sounded like a dream and I remember thinking that someday I would see Venice and have a ride of my own on one of its famous gondolas.

I'm sure it's way more romantic and atmospheric to have a starlit gondola ride down Venice's Grand Canal with your new husband than it is to have a daylight one with three other giggling college students. Since our gondola ride was during mid-afternoon, it was...revealing. About halfway through our ride, Kathy yelled, "Oh wow! Look over my side." There, bobbing along in the water beside her, was a huge turd. It kind of took all the romance out of everything. That was all we needed to set us off in a fit of giggles. Our gondolier must've thought we were completely insane.

A little while later, we caught up to The Katharine Hepburn Clan's gondola. We were shouting happily back and forth to each other over the water when Julie exclaimed, "A condom!" Sure enough, one was floating right by us. Again, we dissolved into giggles.

"Well, girls, at least they were practicing safe sex," observed Katharine Hepburn with a wicked grin and a raised eyebrow. Kathy, Julie, Sharolyn, and I lost any remaining shred of composure and nearly wet our pants.

After the non-stop pace of our Italian trip, it was good to get back to Canterbury and chill out for a couple of days. Kathy, Julie, and Sharolyn were going to the Lake District, and I'd be leaving for Bath, Glastonbury, and Yorkshire. We wouldn't see each other again until classes started up for Trinity term. Before we split up for our travels, the four of us walked into Canterbury for dinner and set a date to have a "picture party," where we'd share our Italian photos and get copies of our favorite shots for each other.

On the walk back up the hill after dinner, Julie asked, "So are you excited to see Sal at Easter?" We hadn't talked about him much while we were in Italy.

"I suppose, but I'm nervous, too – the whole Kevin thing has made the situation with Sal even more complicated. He's spending a lot of money to come over here for just a long weekend. What if things don't go well?"

"There's only one way to find out. You would've had to face each other when you went back to Massachusetts. Maybe it's better to do it now."

"Well, it's too late to change, anyway."

"I'll be thinking of you."

"Thanks."

Before I went to bed, I headed downstairs to say goodbye to Arvine, who was getting ready to leave the next morning for a few days at home in Coventry. She hadn't been in when we set out for the restaurant and I wanted to see her before I left campus again. She answered the door with a warm smile and her usual hug. "What a lovely surprise to see you, Diane – I was afraid I'd missed you."

"I know who *you* must've been with at dinner," I said knowingly, as Arvine went beet-red. She and Bob had been conspicuous in their absence when we'd knocked on their doors to round them up for dinner. They'd begun dating recently.

"So how did you enjoy Italy?" Arvine asked, desperate to change the subject. She was very private and didn't like us making a big deal out of her and Bob. "Kathy says you're all exhausted."

"Oh it was a blast, but I think that on my next coach tour I'm packing my vitamins. It was hard work keeping up with all those senior citizens. They ran us into the ground!"

We sat and chatted for a while, mostly about Arvine's plans for after graduation and what I was going to do when I got back to the States. As I was getting ready to leave, she said, "How do you feel about Sal's visit later this month?"

"Oh, Arvine. I don't want to lead him on and I do care about him. But I kind of wish I hadn't said yes to him flying out."

"Does that have anything to do with Kevin?"

"No. Well, yes, I guess. I don't know. Kevin and I agreed to be just friends, but if I were here longer and Sal wasn't in the picture maybe things would be different. Kevin hasn't come right out and actually said he wants to be with me. But he kissed me at the Rag Ball. I probably shouldn't have let *that* happen, either."

"Diane, I know how confused you are. I'm going to pray for you," Arvine said as we walked across her room to the door and she hugged me goodbye. I was touched by this unexpected gesture. Nobody had ever prayed for me before (not that I knew of, anyway). It was one of the kindest things that anyone had ever done for me.

✧ Chapter Nineteen ✧

It was two days after Easter, and I was on a train bound for the Canterbury West rail station. I had just said goodbye to Sal at Heathrow and had made the long ride back into Central London by Tube to catch my train out to Kent. Classes would be starting soon and I was looking forward to the normal routine again. Mostly, I was relieved that Sal's visit was behind me.

It had been a lot of planning, between finding a hotel, buying theater tickets, making dinner reservations, and creating a sightseeing itinerary. I had wanted everything to be perfect, but of course it wasn't. The minute Sal stepped off the plane and I saw him, I felt awkward. So much had happened in the last six months. If there was any doubt that I was no longer the person he'd said goodbye to at Logan Airport last October, it vanished the minute he saw me.

"Wow – you look so different," he said. "I can't put my finger on it. You're...older, somehow."

I'd purposely made sure our base was in London. Once I'd shown him some of the bigger attractions in the capital, we'd take a day trip to Canterbury, spending Easter Sunday there and attending service in the cathedral. I already knew that all of my English friends would be home with their families and that most of my American friends would still be travelling. It somehow didn't seem right for us to actually stay anywhere near UKC. I think Sal sensed that.

One of the places in London that Sal really wanted to see was Ronnie Scott's Jazz Club, an institution for anyone who loves jazz. Countless legends had performed there. We caught a show at the club on our first night in London, after a fancy dinner at a restaurant in Sloane Square, a very posh part of London.

Ronnie Scott's was like a time-capsule from the 1950s: high-backed round booths, low lighting, and thick clouds of blue-grey cigarette smoke floating in the air. The jazz club, and the London weekend in general, had certainly been a slice of The Good Life: gourmet restaurants, exclusive bars, expensive seats at a performance of "Les Miserables," and first-class train compartments on our day trip to Canterbury.

I should've felt like I'd arrived. Instead, I felt uncomfortable all weekend, like I was pretending to be somebody else or wearing clothes that were a couple of sizes too big for me. It was as if I were trying on somebody else's life – the life of a person who was much older and far more sophisticated than I was.

On Easter Sunday, after I'd shown Sal around Canterbury and the university, we had a fish and chips dinner at one of the cafes near the train station. Then we caught the late train back into London. The next day would be the final one of Sal's stay in England and we had a full schedule of sightseeing planned. I was pretty quiet on the train ride, and my silence didn't go unnoticed for long.

"Diane, I know you worked very hard to make all of these plans," Sal started.

"I did," I interrupted, more forcefully than I'd intended.

"I didn't realize how much pressure I put you under by coming out here," he continued calmly. "It's been a wonderful visit. I'll always remember these past few days. But you have a whole other life back in Canterbury."

"Sal, it's just that there's so much I can't explain to you about being here. You write me these long letters and there are always so many of them. I'm barely keeping up with my schoolwork because I'm off doing so many cool things. I feel like there's no time to write the kinds of letters to you that you write to me. It's — it's — a chore sometimes."

I'd begun to cry. "I feel awful about everything. You're back in Boston, I'm here in England, we didn't make any promises to each other, and it's not fair to either of us to pretend we can just pick up where we left off last fall." I sure wasn't sounding older and sophisticated now. "I'm not even making sense," I cried. "I sound horrible and ungrateful." I had never been so ashamed of myself in my life.

"You're making perfect sense," Sal said. "And you're not horrible or ungrateful." He sat really still and stared out the train window for a long time. Then he spoke again. "Let's make the most of tomorrow, O.K.? After that, I'll be back in Boston and you'll be back in Canterbury. Everyone will be where they're supposed to be."

Know Before You Go

Entangling Alliances: The Ones You Left Behind

In hindsight, I didn't do poor Sal or myself any favors by agreeing to his Easter weekend visit. In the long run, it would've been far better for both of us if we'd simply called it quits before I'd left the U.S. for England.

If you're getting ready for your junior year abroad and you're wondering what to do about your hometown sweetheart, let my misguided decisions be an example. Save yourself and your significant other a lot of drama and heartache; break up before you leave the States. Give yourself the permission you need to be fully and completely present in an experience you worked so hard to earn. And give your partner the freedom that he or she deserves.

Like my mom has always said, "If it's meant to be, it's meant to be." A lot can happen in a year.

Part Three

✧ TRINITY TERM ✧

✧ Chapter Twenty ✧

My third and final term was beginning. In just a couple of short months classes would end for the year, and then I'd have to say goodbye to Canterbury and the friends I'd made. All of the American students were dreading it. Some of us were staying on to make one last trip around Europe before flying home. I'd be one of them; after a lot of hemming and hawing, I'd booked a two-week coach tour to Spain, Portugal, and Morocco. I'd be going by myself, since Julie and Sharolyn were flying back to the States right after classes ended, and Kathy had made other travel plans.

I'd also booked my flight back to Logan Airport. On July 8th I'd be returning to America. But in the meantime, I was determined to enjoy every last second that remained of my junior year abroad. That included the long-awaited, rescheduled Dance to France, which happened on May 2nd.

We ended up raising a lot of money for Save the Children that night. We also drank a lot of beer. By the time our ferry returned from Calais to Dover and we boarded the coaches for the ride back to Canterbury, I was ready to drink something – anything – that didn't have alcohol in it. Kevin saved the day by producing some bottled water from his bag and handing it over to me.

"So did you have a fun time?" he asked as the coaches rolled away from the ferry port and Dover faded into the fog behind us.

"I sure did! Thanks again for buying me the perfume. I love it." He'd impulsively bought me a bottle of Anais Anais (my favorite fragrance) at the duty-free shopping center in Calais. Since the start of Trinity term, he'd been paying quite a bit of attention to me, but nothing had actually happened – we'd simply been spending a lot more time together.

Sometimes it was a walk over to the sports complex, where we'd take an aerobics class. Other times it was a late-night chat over a cup of tea in his room or my room. We even went to the library on a fairly regular basis in the evenings, now that final exams were looming on the horizon. We still hadn't had a serious talk, but it seemed that with Sal's visit in the past, things were more relaxed and a lot less awkward between us.

By the time the coaches dropped everyone off at Keynes, it was nearly 5 am. We were wired from having been up all night, and so Kevin and I ended up back in his room for a pre-dawn cup of tea. And suddenly, it happened.

"Diane, I've cared about you all along," Kevin blurted out. "I could've kicked myself for the way I acted after the Rag Ball and for deciding that we should just be friends. I missed you a lot over the Easter holiday."

"I missed you, too."

"I'm just going to come out and say it. I don't want you to leave and go back to America in July. I want you to stay here as long as you can. I think we should make a go of it and enjoy the time we have left. Let's not even think about having to say good-bye." He pulled me into his arms and began kissing me.

Together we watched the sun rise from Kevin's window. It was one of the few sunrises I'd ever seen. I hadn't been so happy in a long time and I wasn't confused anymore. Kevin squeezed my hand and I turned to smile at him.

"Diane?"

"Yeah?"

"I think I'm falling in love with you."

188

"Thank God!" Kathy yelled. "Crappy timing with only two months left in the year, but thank God all the same. We're really happy for you both."

Kathy, Julie, Sharolyn, and I were sitting in Kathy's room. I'd returned to my own room just after sunrise to catch a few hours' sleep and then a long shower. Then I headed downstairs to see my friends; I told them all about the Dance to France and how Kevin had finally confessed how he felt.

"It's going to be a horror show at the airport when we have to say goodbye in July," I worried. "I mean, I have to go home – it's my senior year at Mount Holyoke. I can't just stay in England." We'd already heard about one American student over here who'd fallen in love with an English guy; they had decided to get married so she could stay in the U.K. As much as I loved this country and cared for Kevin, I knew I had to finish my degree at home.

"Don't worry about all that stuff," Julie said. "It's going to take care of itself. You can see each other over Christmas and spring breaks once you're back at Mount Holyoke. You two are SO CUTE together! We knew this would happen!"

"You make us sound like a pair of Yorkshire terriers."

"Oh come on, Diane," Sharolyn chimed in. "We're just glad that you and Kevin have finally figured out what we already knew months ago. You're perfect for each other."

"Hey, will you introduce Kevin to your parents next week?" Kathy asked.

"As a matter of fact, we're driving into Heathrow to pick them up so we can take them over to the car rental place. So yes, they'll meet him."

"They're going to love him," Julie gushed. "Who wouldn't?" My parents were arriving in a few days for a two-week stay in England. I hadn't seen them since they'd put me on the plane to London last October, and I couldn't wait to be with them. My dad, an avid marathoner, was going to be running the London Marathon, and my mom and I were going to stand on Tower Bridge and cheer him on.

After the London Marathon, my parents were going to drive out to Canterbury so that I could show them around the city and introduce them to everyone. We were also going to yell for Kevin, Julie, Ian, and Sharolyn as they ran the Canterbury Half-Marathon. After that, I'd be blowing off classes for a couple of days so that I could travel with my parents up to Cambridge. It was going to be a busy couple of weeks.

"I hope they like him. You're all going to come out for dinner with us one night while they're in Canterbury, right? My parents really want to try Indian food. Oh, and my dad is bringing some of those cool Mylar running blankets for you guys when you run the half-marathon. He got them at the Boston Marathon last month. Won't that be neat?"

"I still can't believe your dad runs marathons, Diane," Kathy said. "My dad doesn't even run down the driveway."

"Yeah, he's hooked — I'm afraid all I ever did was the two-mile on my high school's track team. Maybe someday. Hey, I'm starving - what do you say we find Colin and see if he's interested in going out for a pub lunch?"

My parents had the time of their lives on their visit to England. I don't think they slept a whole lot during their stay, since they were busy trying to see as much as possible while they were here. Echoing Warren Zevon, my dad always says, "You can sleep when you're dead." My mom had to insist that he get one decent rest the night before the marathon.

On the day of the London Marathon, my mom and I couldn't believe we were really standing on Tower Bridge together waiting for my dad to run by. We'd told him exactly where we'd be, and he actually spotted us first. I'd only ever watched the Boston Marathon before, and I always enjoyed it – but to have London's skyline stretched out in front of and behind us, with the Thames underneath us, was an incredible experience.

After the marathon, my parents drove out to Canterbury in their rental car. I'd booked them into a hotel in the city center and went down to meet them once they'd arrived.

"So how did Dad do on the left side of the road?" I asked my mom. "You guys don't look too stressed out." I'd now lived here seven months and still couldn't imagine driving on the other side of the road. It had taken me ages to get the hang of looking right-left-right when I was walking across a street, and that had been hairy enough in the beginning.

"He did beautifully," my mom answered. "I don't know how he managed to find his way out of London and on to Canterbury, but we made it in one piece." The car GPS was still nearly 20 years in the future, so my parents had to make do with good old-fashioned maps.

Funnily enough, my dad's only scary driving moment in England was late one night when they were driving me up the hill and back to the university after dinner. There was a mini-roundabout at the bottom of the hill which my dad entered without incident. For some reason, though, when he came out of the roundabout, he went to the right-hand side of the road. It was only a split-second, but it seemed to last forever.

"Other side, Dad!" I screamed as I saw my short life flash before my eyes. "Other side!!"

"Jesus, Mary, and Joseph!" my mom cried in a half-yell, half-prayer. Fortunately for us, the Holy Family, and everyone else, the roads were quiet that night and nobody was heading towards us down the hill.

"I don't know what the hell happened back there," my dad said as he shook his head. "I was doing great up until then."

"Never mind, Dad. Let's just make sure that you and Mom live to tell about your trip. No going home with anything in a cast."

My parents' visit was over way too fast. Before I knew it, I was saying goodbye to them at Heathrow.

"It was so good to finally see you, honey," my mom said as she hugged me. "Daddy and I loved meeting all of your friends and visiting Canterbury. We can see why you love it here so much." Whether it was intentional or not, she looked at Kevin, who was standing at my side and holding my hand.

My dad stepped forward and shook Kevin's free hand before giving me one last hug. "We'll see you in July, Dee – just make the most of your last two months here. Do everything you want to do and go everywhere you want to go before you have to come home. Remember...."

"I know, Dad," I said with a smile, because I already knew what he was about to say. "I can sleep when I'm dead."

Mom and Dad Giombetti in tiny Mercery Lane, with Christchurch Gate and the cathedral in the background.

The beautiful gardens along the Cambridge Backs.

✧ Chapter Twenty-Two ✧

With the end of Trinity term and the school year fast
approaching, most of my spare time was spent trying to cram
important "lasts" in before my final exams – a last Sunday pub
lunch with Colin, a last session on the Stour with the men's four,
a last visit to the cathedral for evensong, a last day trip into
London, a last walk to The Dog and Bear with Arvine and the
gang, and a last evening of ballroom dancing at King's Hall.

It was sinking in that my junior year abroad was almost over,
and I was not happy about it. One night in late May after trying
(unsuccessfully) to study for one of my upcoming exams, I wrote
the following in my journal:

> *I really don't want to go home. I feel so settled in here, like*
> *I belong, and the thought of leaving everyone, especially my*
> *British friends, really bums me out big time. I can't stand*
> *thinking about it at all. What am I going to do next year?*
> *Mount Holyoke will be the same as it's always been, the*
> *people will be the same, and all my friends will be the same.*
> *I've changed so much and experienced so many new things,*
> *but when I go home it'll be just like I never left. What a*
> *depressing thought.*

And speaking of depressing, there were final exams to
get through, and they were nothing like the self-scheduled
privileges I enjoyed at Mount Holyoke. At UKC, we were told
when to show up for each of our final exams. They all took
place in the huge gymnasium inside the sports complex where we
went for aerobics classes. Row after row of evenly spaced desks
and chairs – hundreds of them – covered the floor in an enormous
grid pattern.

You showed up on your appointed date at the appointed hour and sat your exam with loads of other people at the same time. You were assigned to a certain desk in the gymnasium. You were allowed to bring snacks and a pen or pencil into the room with you, and nothing else (I half-expected to get patted down by a security guard before being allowed in). Your specific subject's exam was handed to you as you registered for your exam in the gymnasium's lobby. The stress in the gymnasium was palpable.

I personally had a huge problem with the snacks-allowed policy. At every single one of my four exams, I had the exceedingly bad luck to be seated near some idiot who cracked his gum or loudly unwrapped and then slurped on hard candies for the duration of the exam. I came out of each exam with a splitting headache.

Worse still, the exams were proctored. Walking up and down between the rows of desks were invigilators. Some of the invigilators walked very slowly and paused to look over your shoulder at what you were writing (pretty irritating), some of them paced frantically as if their pants were on fire (really distracting) and one particularly annoying invigilator jingled the change in his pocket non-stop while he walked up and down between the rows of desks near me. I wanted to jump up out of my chair and strangle him.

Say what? **Brit/Yank Translator**	**Proctored**: *monitored* **Invigilators**: *Men and women who patrol the examination room. They watch for any sign of cheating or writing after the "pens down" command.*

All in all, the final exam experience was a downer. It seemed to assume that you were out to cheat, and it bore no resemblance whatsoever to the Mount Holyoke exam experience, which was almost spa-like in comparison. At Mount Holyoke, we had self-scheduled exams; you decided when you took your exams during finals week. As long as you were finished by the end of exam week, it didn't matter which days you took which exams. Even better, you could take your exams in any number of academic buildings on campus. The college's Honor Code meant that there was no need for invigilators; nobody would dream of cheating, because abusing the Honor Code meant that we'd have the privilege of self-scheduled exams taken away.

With our exams behind us, all we had to do now was enjoy the rest of our junior year abroad. Kathy, Julie, Sharolyn, Bob, and I decided to have a final evening with Arvine and the gang the night before our English friends left UKC for good. We'd planned a "farewell banquet" on my corridor's kitchenette that consisted of chocolate-chip pancakes with gin and tonics.

It was no Thanksgiving feast, but it was one of our more creative meals. We took tons of photos of each other, exchanged addresses and phone numbers, and promised to write, call, and visit as often as we could. Arvine was thinking about a Christmastime trip to see Bob in Indiana, and Kathy and I were lucky enough that we'd be only a short bus ride apart when we returned to UMASS and Mount Holyoke in the fall. There were lots of tears and hugs. I knew that saying goodbye wouldn't be fun, but I didn't think it would be this hard.

It was equally difficult to say so long to my rowing and ballroom dancing friends. We'd all shared so much with each other during the past year, and although I'd only been friends with them since last fall, it felt as if I'd known them much longer than that.

"So my little Di-ah-na," Amatsia said as he caught me in a huge bear hug the night I said goodbye to him and the rest of the guys in the rowing club. "Will you use your big voice in the boats at Mount Holyoke?"

"Oh, I don't think so, Amatsia. How could I follow this act? Nothing would ever come close." It wasn't far from the truth. Mount Holyoke's rowing team was just that – a fiercely competitive, highly skilled, and nationally ranked team. Although I'd enjoyed every minute of my short-lived coxing career in England, I already knew I didn't want the pressure of practicing every day at dawn as the crew team at Mount Holyoke did.

As far as I knew, there would be no ballroom dancing for me at Mount Holyoke, either. That would have to wait until my first visit back to UKC. I'd already been thinking about when that might be. If I worked enough hours at my campus jobs at Mount Holyoke, I'd have enough money saved up for a trip during spring break of my senior year.

"Maybe I can dance with all of you as a special guest next spring when I come out to visit," I joked. "Perhaps the ballroom dancing club would be so kind as to arrange an evening at King's Hall for me for old time's sake." We all laughed, but it killed me to know that I wouldn't be there to dance with all of my friends every week next year. And I didn't even want to think about Kevin having another partner.

Kevin and I had successfully postponed having to say goodbye...which was a huge relief to both of us. Our plan was to travel around England and possibly some of France for a couple of weeks once I'd returned from my coach tour of Spain, Portugal, and Morocco. We'd use his parents' house in Petersfield as a base, and then Kevin would take me to the airport in July for my flight back to Logan.

And then there was Colin – it was especially tough to say goodbye to him. He'd been the first English person I'd met on campus, and without him I would've been completely lost those first couple of weeks.

"I hate goodbyes," I said to him on my last visit to his flat in Parkwood. "You know I'll be back as soon as I can. Trouble is, I won't get to see you here." Colin had already landed his first job, an entry-level position at an insurance company in London.

"Never mind, Diane – I have a feeling we won't lose touch anytime soon."

"I'm so glad Allison introduced us. I don't know what I would've done without you."

"Well, if we'd never met, I suppose you never would've been almost knocked up, would you?" He gave me a dirty grin.

"Fresh!" I said as I swatted his arm and then hugged him.

✧ Chapter Twenty-Three ✧

On June 6th, I began my two-week coach tour through
Spain, Portugal, and Morocco. As much as I would've loved to
travel completely on my own, I was a little worried about the
language barrier these destinations presented. My Spanish was
nonexistent, and my Portuguese consisted of only two things
I'd learned as a little girl from my Nina: "underpants" and
"come here". I didn't think either one would be terribly useful
on the road. As far as Morocco, I didn't know a word of Arabic,
but I would be able to use my French; however, we wouldn't be
visiting Morocco until the end of the trip. So a coach tour it was.

I wondered what kind of a roommate I'd have. I wasn't
about to pay an expensive supplement for a single, and I'd
never get to know my fellow travelers that way. So I put in for a
roommate assignment, made sure to write my age on the form,
and crossed my fingers. If this coach tour was anything like our
Italian one, I'd be the youngest person on it. My roommate
ended up being Barbara, a middle-aged English woman who
was old enough to be my mom. Unfortunately for me, she was
also a chain-smoker.

As far as I could gather, roommate assignments on coach
tours appear to be made as arbitrarily as roommate assignments
in college are made. In other words, nobody seemed to pay
attention to the section on the form where you say whether
you're a night owl, early riser, party animal, wallflower,
smoker, or non-smoker. Barbara and I couldn't have been
more different.

Inexplicably, our tour company had made a second "Odd
Couple" roommate assignment on the tour. They had paired up

Joan, another middle-aged, chain-smoking English woman, with Bibi, a non-smoking American college student who'd just finished her junior year abroad at Cambridge. By the second day of the tour, we had corrected the roommate situation. Barbara was sharing a room with Joan, I was sharing with Bibi, and everybody was much happier.

Bibi's real name was Rukhsana and she was of Indian descent. She'd grown up in California, and her parents were former flower children who'd been at the original Woodstock. Bibi was a self-described "vegetarian hippie health-nut" who just happened to speak Spanish. Since she had beautiful dark skin, hair, and eyes, the Spanish all thought Bibi was one of them, and spoke their native language to her at warp-speed. She tried her best to teach me a few useful travel phrases. The only one I still remembered by the end of the trip was, "*Es con sel?*" (More or less translated as, "Does that have salt in it?")

Spain was the first country on our tour, and Madrid was our first stop. I was surprised at how many gypsies there were in the city. One side of the hotel we were staying in overlooked a vacant lot where some gypsy families had set up a rough camp. At dusk on our first day, I happened to be looking out the window of our hotel room when I saw one of the gypsy women leave her shack and walk over to a far corner of the lot. She just squatted down, lifted her skirts, and did her business right there in full view of anyone who happened to be nearby. I was aghast.

We had a pretty fun mix of couples and singles on our tour, with one notable exception. A group of four English ladies –

senior citizens – were booked on the tour with us, and they were the polar opposite of my beloved Katharine Hepburn Clan from the Italy tour. These women were the stereotypical "old-lady Brit abroad." From the minute they came down to breakfast until the moment they said goodnight and headed off to their rooms, all these gals did was whine and complain. They bellyached about the food (too spicy), the weather (too hot), and the natives (too loud). Nobody wanted to sit with them at the family-style mealtimes, and there was always a mad rush to whichever tables were farthest away from where "the old whiners" were.

"If I ever get like that, I hope somebody slaps me," Barbara cracked one night at dinner. Barbara, Joan, Bibi, and I ate together at most meals and had become pretty friendly.

"No worries there, Barbara," Bibi answered. "You are nothing like them." We began to wonder why the old whiners had left their safe cocoon of England at all – they certainly didn't seem to be enjoying themselves and were making no attempts to experience the local culture. Most everyone else on the tour, on the other hand, jumped right in with both feet. We haggled with street vendors in the medina at Fez, went swimming at the local beaches in Malaga, asked for directions to the Alfama district restaurants where the tourists didn't typically go, and signed up for camel rides.

The coolest thing that happened to me on the tour took place on my first night in Portugal. It had been an early morning wakeup call in Spain, followed by tons of driving time;

202

before we'd even arrived in Portugal, we'd already covered a lot of road. We stopped for short visits in Avila and then Salamanca, Spain. As we finally entered Portugal at its northernmost tip, we navigated narrow passes in the Riff Mountains and crisscrossed the magnificent Serra da Estrela (Portuguese for "star") Mountains.

The terrain was amazing, with green peaks rising and falling all around us. At some points, our coach crossed valleys using long overpasses that were high above the ground – like a Disneyworld monorail, only much higher up. Trees, mountains, and valleys stretched for as far as the eye could see.

Our final stop for the rest of that day and night was a small hotel in a beautiful mountaintop village near Coimbra, a university city. Thanks to our early morning start, Bibi and I had a little time to explore the village before we had to return to the hotel for our dinner. It was gorgeous, with lots of tiny bars, interesting shops that sold locally made jewelry and other crafts, and side streets packed with stucco and tile-decorated houses. The people here were incredibly friendly, more so than in Madrid, I thought, and I wished we were spending more than just one evening.

After dinner, I went up to our room, got my journal, and headed back down to the hotel's main lounge. It was cozy, with small tables scattered around the room and some sofas and a TV in the center. The lounge was deserted. Our tour group had almost taken over the hotel and it had been a long travel day, so most people had already turned in for the night. Bibi wanted to sleep, but I wasn't tired, so here I was. I sat down at one of the tables and began to write.

After a while, a middle-aged man walking with the aid of a cane entered the room. He was extremely well dressed in a suit that must've been custom tailored for his large frame. If this had been America, I'd have pegged him as a former NFL player, although his tinted eyeglasses made him look more like a secret agent from a spy movie. He walked around the room with a grumpy expression and inspected everything in the lounge; light fixtures, tabletops, the books on the shelves. I didn't recognize him from our tour group, so I figured he must be a business traveler and went back to writing in my journal.

Suddenly he was at my side and speaking Portuguese really rapidly. He appeared to be asking me a question. I caught the word "Portuguese" and it dawned on me that he might be asking if I spoke the language. *Oh great – a lonely businessman trying to pick up girls*, I thought. *Maybe I should go back up to my room after all.* But for some reason, I didn't. Instead, I shook my head and said in English, "No Portuguese. I'm American. Do you speak English?"

The man looked disappointed and shook his head, but instead of leaving, he just stood there looking at me, as if he were waiting for something to happen. On a long shot, I said a few words in the only other language I knew: French. I took a deep breath and said, *"Je parle un peu de francais, monsieur. Et vous?"* (I speak a little French, sir. And you?)

The man's face lit up with a huge smile. He removed his glasses and reached out to shake my hand enthusiastically. *"Oui! Oui! Je parle francais aussi. Y-a-t'il quelqu'un ici avec vous?"* (Yes! Yes! I speak French, too. Is there anyone here with you?) He motioned to the empty seat at my table. When I shook my head no, he sat down opposite me and propped his cane against the wall.

For almost two hours, the man and I chatted away in French. Alvaro, as he introduced himself, turned out not to be a passing business traveler at all – he was the owner of our hotel! A waiter from the hotel's restaurant nervously scurried over to Alvaro as soon as he sat down, and appeared to be asking him if the two of us would like anything.

"*Mademoiselle*, I insist you try the famous Vinho Verde, which you must drink when you're in Portugal. Please be my guest," Alvaro said gallantly. I certainly wasn't going to pass up drinks on the house and our tour guide had said during today's long drive that drinking Vinho Verde was a must.

Alvaro didn't seem to mind my imperfect French, and he spoke slowly and clearly so that I could understand his Portuguese-accented French. After a few minutes (and a few sips of wine), I overcame my self-consciousness and started thinking how happy Mrs. Carey, my favorite French teacher from Ashland High School, would be if she could see me now. This was pretty cool. Two complete strangers, neither of whom spoke each other's native languages, were conversing in a common third language.

"You speak French very well, *mademoiselle*," Alvaro said. "Where did you learn to speak? And how long have you known the language?"

I did some quick math in my head. "I began learning in secondary school, *monsieur*. This is my ninth year speaking French and I will take my university degree in English and French literature next year," I replied.

"*Bon.* You are intelligent, then. What brought you to Portugal, and why are you so far from America?"

I told Alvaro how I'd come to England on my junior year abroad and explained that our exams had just finished. "I picked this trip because the countries are ones that I've never visited before, and because one of my grandmothers is Portuguese. Her parents – my great-grandparents – came to America from Portugal. From the Azores, actually."

"Ah, that is wonderful. You are Portuguese by descent. That is why you are so lovely. And what do you think of our beautiful country so far?"

"I like it very much," I replied, and told him everything we'd seen on the drive from Spain. He nodded thoughtfully as I described our trip through the mountain passes and chuckled when I told him how unusual it was to American eyes to see men and women on the roads driving carts pulled by oxen and donkeys. The French words for these animals temporarily slipped my mind, so I substituted *"vaches"* (cows) and *"chevaux"* (horses) instead. But Alvaro got my drift nevertheless.

"Portugal has the lowest individual income among all the European countries right now," he informed me. "For example, the average Spanish person earns 6-8 times the monthly income of the average Portuguese person. In many ways our country is behind the times. But we have a rich maritime history and we were once a huge empire and a nation of explorers. In America you learned about our brave *conquistadores*, perhaps?"

Yes, I knew about them. In sixth grade, we'd spent an entire month learning all about the mighty Portuguese navy and the great empire they'd built. And we'd studied all the names and routes of the Portuguese *conquistadores*. I named as many as I could remember off the top of my head, and told Alvaro how much I was looking forward to seeing Lisbon, from where so many of the explorers had launched their voyages. He was impressed that I knew some of his country's history.

"Being a hotel owner must be interesting," I said. "You must meet lots of people in your work."

"Yes, and it is a good living, with business from tourists who are coming into Portugal from Spain," Alvaro replied. "I can provide jobs to many people who live in this village. This and my other work keep me busy." At this point, Alvaro reached into his jacket pocket, took a business card from a leather case, and gave it to me. It listed the hotel's address and phone number, with his name and title in prominent type. Printed in the bottom-right corner of the card in much smaller type were an address and phone number in nearby Coimbra.

"This is my business card for the hotel, but I also consult at the university in Coimbra, as well as for the local tourist board. If you would like to learn Portuguese, it would be my pleasure to suggest that you study at our university once you are finished with your studies in America. You may contact me and I will personally help you arrange it."

"That is very kind of you, *monsieur*. Thank you. I have not yet decided what I'd like to do after I leave university. There are a lot of choices." I wasn't lying; I hadn't a clue what I wanted to do with my life after leaving Mount Holyoke. Grad school? A real job? Backpacking around the world? It was kind of overwhelming, to tell the truth.

At this, Alvaro looked sad. I worried that I'd unintentionally offended him by brushing off his kind offer. Then he began to talk again. He said that he'd lived all his life in Coimbra, where he'd met his wife. They'd married and had a child, and were very happy together. One night, when Alvaro was still a young father, his wife and child died in a car accident. He told the story with very little show of emotion on his face, but his hands trembled as he spoke.

"I am so very sorry, *monsieur*," I said. "How sad to lose your family. You must miss them a great deal."

"I do not tell you my story to make you sad, *mademoiselle*. I tell you because it is important for you to make the most of your opportunities. You are so young and you have only one life – you must make it a good one, however long or short it is. Life is a gift." He brightened up at this, and said, "It would be my honor to give you an evening tour of the village and Coimbra. My personal driver will take us. With your permission, of course." He looked at me hopefully.

The offer was tempting – here was an opportunity to see the area with a local expert. But this man was a total stranger, after all. What if he ordered his driver to pull into some remote clearing in the middle of nowhere and then attacked me? It could happen. What if the story about his dead wife and child was just that – a story? I erred on the side of caution and politely declined, apologizing to Alvaro and telling him that I was exhausted from the day's journey and was ready to go upstairs to sleep.

He nodded understandingly. "Do not apologize. You are a wise girl. I will escort you upstairs." Together we walked to the lobby and entered the tiny elevator. When we got to my floor,

Alvaro pressed the "Open Door" button, held it in, and squeezed my hand tightly. He had tears in his eyes. "You made an old man very happy tonight. Thank you for spending time with me." He bent down and kissed me on the cheek, and I stepped out of the elevator. Then Alvaro closed the elevator door and was gone.

Chapter Twenty-Four

On June 20th, I arrived back in London and said goodbye to all of my traveling companions from the tour. Bibi and I exchanged addresses so that we could keep in touch once we both got back to the States. From Heathrow I took the Tube into central London and caught the first train out to Canterbury West, where Kevin would pick me up at the station.

There were now about three weeks left in my junior year abroad. Arriving back at the university drove the point home. The campus was really quiet; many of the regular students had gone home for the summer, and the Americans were either traveling or already back home in the States.

"Wow, this is depressing," I said to Kevin as he helped me take my suitcases back to my room. My corridor was completely silent. There didn't appear to be anybody left. On the bright side, that meant I wouldn't have to wait ages for a washing machine or a dryer. "I'll tell you what I'm not going to miss about this place," I said to Kevin as I began unpacking and sorting my dirty laundry into loads. "Laundry room stress – and hoarding my 50p and 10p coins for the washer and dryer."

"Why don't you just wait until we get to my parents' house?" Kevin suggested. "You can do your washing there."

"No, I don't want to impose. Besides, if I don't do it today I'll have nothing left for tomorrow. I'm wearing the last of my clean things. It was so hot in Morocco that we went through two changes of clothes every day."

"Well, why don't you come find me when you're done, then? You're going to need some help getting all of those boxes to the Post Office in Canterbury."

Before I'd left for my tour, I'd carefully wrapped and boxed up all of my books, papers, folders, posters, knickknacks and memorabilia, as well as the hundreds of photos I'd taken. They were too bulky and heavy to cart home in my suitcases, so I was going to ship them back to the U.S. via surface mail (boat). It was much cheaper than air mail. I also simply didn't have the suitcase space – I'd managed to accumulate an impressive amount of new clothes and shoes over the past nine months.

That night, after I'd returned from the Post Office, had dinner, and come back from visiting Kevin in C Block, I stood in the middle of my dorm room and looked around me. Now that I'd shipped everything home except for the essentials, G2-2 was as bare as I'd first found it last October. But although it was emptied of things, the room was still full – of memories. It was a good feeling.

Two days later, we crammed Kevin's car to the bursting point with my remaining things and the contents of his study bedroom. Then we went to the Keynes Porter's Office to turn in our keys and leave UKC.

"This feels weird, huh?" I asked Kevin as we each signed the forms acknowledging that we'd officially vacated our rooms.

"Yes – but it was a good year, wasn't it? And we still have a fun two weeks to look forward to. I can't wait for you to meet all of my mates from home. I'm really glad you decided not to go back to America until July, Diane."

"Me too." We walked back to the car and got ready for the 90-minute drive to Petersfield.

"There's your last look at the cathedral," Kevin said as we drove away from campus and headed out of Canterbury for the motorway. "Wave goodbye, now."

"Oh don't say that! I'll start to cry. You make it sound as if I'll never be back again." But I waved anyhow. I kept my eyes fixed on the cathedral until it was nothing but a tiny speck on the horizon that finally vanished from sight. I felt like I was saying goodbye to an old friend.

"I hope your friends from home like me," I worried as we arrived in Petersfield. I'd already met Kevin's parents, younger brother, and Nana when they'd come out to visit a couple of weeks after my own parents had visited. I guess I'd made a good enough impression, since his mum and dad were having me to stay in their home between the trips that Kevin and I had planned.

"My friends are going to love you," Kevin reassured me. "Just like I do. Stop worrying. Well, we're here – 3 Love Lane."

We pulled into a driveway and in front of a large brick home that was almost completely hidden from the street by a tall, thick wall of evergreen trees. Wisteria covered part of the front of the house. There were flowers, ornamental grasses, decorative borders, and blooming shrubs everywhere I looked. And that was just in the front yard.

"Oh wow – my Grampa would love this!" I gasped as we stepped out of the car. "He's a huge gardener. I'll have to take some pictures so I can show him when I get back."

The house itself was detached and in the middle of its own plot of land, as were all the other houses on this end of Love

Lane. There weren't any semi-detached or terrace houses to be seen. This was obviously an upscale neighborhood. One thing about Kevin's house struck me as a little odd, though. There were two front doors, each with its own mail slot.

"I thought you said this was a detached house," I asked Kevin. "So why are there two front doors?"

"The main part of the house is where my parents and brother live. The other front door closest to the garage leads to the granny annex, where my Nana lives. Here's my mum now. Get ready for lots of hugs. Hi, Mum!"

Say what? Brit/Yank Translator | Granny annex: *in-law apartment*

"Welcome home, darling!" Kevin's mother said as she walked out the front door and came over to give him a bear hug. "Did you have a good trip from Canterbury? Hello, Diane – it's lovely to see you again," she continued as she hugged me next. She walked up to Kevin's car, peered into the back windows, and laughed. "My goodness, would you look at that? I don't think there's any spare room left in there."

"Mum, Diane's quite taken with the front garden," Kevin said. "Shall we show her the back garden? I'll unpack the car later."

Say what? Brit/Yank Translator | Front garden: *front yard*

"That sounds lovely. I'll come out with some cups of tea for everyone in a moment. How do you take yours, Diane?"

"Um, milk no sugar, please. Thank you." Kevin's mum nodded and then went back into the house.

"Come on – I'll show you our back garden. That's the 'back yard' in Yank, isn't it?" Kevin said as he led me over to the side of the house and around what appeared to be a large sunroom.

"Yes it is, smart-ass. But I think 'garden' is a much more appropriate word, if your back one is anything like the front one. Who does all the planting, weeding, and lawn-mowing, anyhow? I'll bet this is a full-time job."

"Not quite. My granddad comes a couple of times a week and does all the gardening. He's retired. And he lives in a caravan park, so he has barely any garden of his own. Here we are – the back garden."

Say what?
Brit/Yank Translator

Caravan park:
trailer park

"Oh my God, Kevin, this is gorgeous! It's unbelievable." I honestly didn't know where to look first. The word "yard" was an insult. I'd already learned from my months in England that this is a nation of gardeners. The Brits have practically taken gardening to the level of a professional sport. To say that it is a national passion is not exaggerating.

Kevin's parents' back garden was like something out of the pages of a magazine, and it was even more spectacular than the front garden. A beautiful flagstone patio came off the back of the house, complete with outdoor furniture and edged with terracotta pots that were filled with annuals. A matching flagstone walkway led from the patio and effectively cut the back garden into two sections.

To the right of the walkway, a small flight of flagstone steps descended to a large vegetable garden, which I immediately checked out. It was extremely tidy, with several rows of plants that were neatly staked, tied, and labeled. I saw potatoes, carrots, parsnips, onions, something that Kevin called "runner beans," and mint. What I didn't see was a single weed. Near the vegetable garden, there were a greenhouse, a shed, and a composting area.

Say what?
Brit/Yank Translator

Runner beans:
string beans

To the left of the walkway was a perfect lawn – there wasn't a blade of crabgrass or a dandelion in sight. An arbor and a trellis, covered with pink, yellow, and peach climbing roses, had been built where the patio led down the stairs to the vegetable garden.

The flagstone walkway led to the far end of the back garden, where there were not one, but two fish ponds, complete with water lily plants and loads of goldfish and koi. There were all different varieties and sizes: solid black, white, gold, and orange, as well as speckled "mongrels." Some were as large as my hand, and others were no bigger than my pinkie finger.

Not far from one of the fish ponds stood an old-fashioned,

stone barbecue that was like the one at my Grampa's house. Borders and flower beds edged much of the lawn, and the entire back garden was planted on all three sides with different evergreen trees and hedges. They had grown so high and close together that you could barely see the roofs of the neighbors' houses in the back and to the sides.

Kevin's mum had appeared on the patio with a tray full of mugs of tea and biscuits. I went back to join her and Kevin at the table.

"Mum, I think Diane's a bit gobsmacked by the garden," Kevin said. "I've never seen her so quiet."

Say what?
Brit/Yank Translator | **Gobsmacked**: *speechless*

"It's so pretty," I said. It was the best I could do – I was still trying to take everything in. "Was all of this here when you bought the house?" I remember Kevin saying that his parents had moved to Love Lane from across town when he was much younger.

"Oh good heavens, no," his mum answered. "You should've seen the state it was in when we bought it. There was nothing here in the way of gardens or landscaping. It was quite bare. Everything was done gradually over the years. The fish ponds are the most recent addition – Kevin's dad built them a couple of years ago."

"Remember what the house looked like when we moved in,

Mum?" Kevin chimed in. He looked at me. "Diane, it was just a box – there was no garage or granny annex back then, and no sunroom. My brother and I helped with some of the building projects. It was good fun, although I'm not sure that Mum and Dad would use the word 'help' to describe everything that Martin and I did."

"Hmmm…that sounds familiar. One of *my* mom's favorite phrases when my sisters and I were little was, 'You wanna help? *Don't* help!' "

"Yes, I think mums all over the world can agree on that," Kevin's mum said with a smile. "So Kev tells me that the two of you have a few trips planned before you head back to the States. I expect you won't be stopping in Petersfield too long."

Uh-oh. This was awkward – Kevin had only just arrived home for the summer, and I'm sure his mum was looking forward to catching up with him. The last thing I wanted to do was make her feel like I was trying to steal her son away from her. But we'd already planned our trips to Oxford and Stratford and booked the B+Bs. And the flights and hotel for Paris were bought and paid for, too. We couldn't exactly change our plans now.

Kevin deftly stepped in and saved me. "Now Mum, I'll be here for the whole summer. Diane's only here 'til the 8th of July and I want to make sure she enjoys the rest of her time in England. We won't be leaving on our Grand Tour for another few days, anyway."

"Oh, well that's all right, then," his mother replied. "It would've been a shame to miss your favorite dinners and puddings, wouldn't it? It's homemade steak and kidney pie followed by lemon crunch tonight. There might even be a shepherd's pie tomorrow night."

Say what?
Brit/Yank Translator

Puddings: *desserts*

"Oh, well done, Mum!" Kevin said happily.

"As a matter of fact," his mum said as she reached for the tea tray and rose from her seat, "I'd better get on with the dinner if we want to eat at a decent time this evening. Excuse me, won't you?" She went back into the house.

"Didn't you tell your mom that we'd be traveling?" I whispered as soon as we were alone on the patio.

"Of course I did. That's just how she is – she's perfectly fine with us going away. Are you almost finished with your tea? That car's not going to unpack itself."

After dinner that night, we walked over to Kevin's local – The Red Lion – to meet up with his friends, who had also just returned home for the summer. They were already there waiting for us when we walked in. There were lots of excited shouts of, "All right, mate?!" and claps on the back.

Kevin made the introductions: there was Andy, one of the tallest guys I'd ever met; Simon, an aspiring musician who constantly drummed his fingers on the tabletop and couldn't sit still; Barry, who resembled Kevin so much that he could've been a blond version of him; Trevor, who was mad about motorcycles and cars; and Mark, who had piercing blue eyes and a meticulously groomed flat-top haircut. They immediately made me feel welcome.

As we all sat down and started chatting with each other, though, I noticed that Mark, who was seated directly across the table from me, was staring at my mouth. *I know I brushed my teeth before we came out*, I thought, *so I can't have food stuck in them. What the hell is he staring at?* It was kind of unnerving. I decided to call him on it.

"O.K., Mark, I give up. What are you staring at?" I asked.

"Your teeth," he replied immediately, not the least bit taken aback by my directness. "They're perfect. Are all Americans' teeth that perfect?"

"Bloody Mark!" Kevin guffawed, as everyone else at the table started to crack up, too. "Steady on, mate – you're going to frighten her!"

My orthodontist, Dr. Chyten, would've been flattered.

Chapter Twenty-Five

"You know what I think?" I said to Kevin over lunch at
The Eagle and Child pub in Oxford (definitely my favorite
British pub name ever). The day before that, we'd eaten lunch
at the nearby Lamb and Flag (my second-favorite British pub
name ever).

"Do I have a choice?" he replied with a smirk.

"No. I was thinking that you're being an awfully good
sport about our Grand Tour. It's a culture-vulture's and
English major's dream rolled into one. Sort of your vision of
hell, isn't it?"

"Well, it's not the kind of holiday I'd choose for myself.
But it's fun to watch you get so excited about everything. And I
will have my lads' holiday in Spain later in the summer. I can
promise you there won't be the slightest bit of culture on that
one. Just lots of beer."

Say what?
Brit/Yank Translator | **Holiday:** *vacation*

"O.K., that evens things out, then. But seriously, Kevin,
thanks for traveling with me. I'm having so much fun. And
secretly, I think you're enjoying all of the culture and just won't
admit to it on principle."

"Well, maybe I'm enjoying it a *little* bit. Just don't
tell anybody."

"Your secret's safe with me."

The Grand Tour had started off with a visit to Oxford. I began by dragging Kevin around the town to see the major sights that were featured in *Oxford Blues*. On a decidedly more highbrow note, we also went on a walking tour of the town and its beautiful colleges. And we visited the university's famous Bodleian Library and Ashmolean Museum. Unlike UKC, Oxford University is absolutely ancient – some of its colleges, like Balliol and Oriel, were founded in the thirteenth and fourteenth centuries.

Just thinking of the generations of great minds that had come out of this place was staggering. Its alumni and faculty included British prime ministers, international heads of state, Nobel Prize laureates, monarchs, saints, Archbishops of Canterbury, and Olympic medal winners. Famous Oxford graduates and instructors from the 20th and 21st centuries alone include physicist Stephen Hawking, comedian Rowan Atkinson (Mr. Bean), former Prime Minister of Pakistan Benazir Bhutto, former Indian Prime Minister Indira Ghandi, and Monty Python member Michael Palin. That is some seriously distinguished company.

Oxford is stunningly beautiful – it's sometimes called "The City of Dreaming Spires." After Kevin and I saw the view from the top of the university's Sheldonian Theatre, we understood why. Spread out below us were the lacy spires of the colleges. It was as if dozens of cathedrals and castles lay at our feet. The place is an architecture nut's dream. There's even a Bridge of Sighs (albeit one that spans a street, not a canal) that is a faithful reproduction of the original that I saw in Venice.

Oxford and its dreaming spires.

It was hard to leave Oxford, but we still had the rest of the Grand Tour ahead of us. Our next stop was Blenheim Palace, the seat of the Dukes of Marlborough. It had been Kevin's only request when we had sat down to plan the Tour weeks before.

"Why Blenheim Palace?" I had asked him as I pored over my *Let's Go.*

"Because it's the birthplace of Winston Churchill," he had answered quickly. Churchill was one of Kevin's heroes. He'd once told me that if he could go back in time and have dinner with any historical figure, he'd choose Winston Churchill. As if to make the visit to Blenheim Palace sound more appealing to me, Kevin had casually thrown in, "Churchill had an American mum, you know."

"No way! I didn't know that. Seriously? You're not pulling my leg, right?"

"I'm quite serious. Despite such an unfortunate start in life, he went on to achieve greatness." He had laughed as I scowled at him. "And I wasn't making that up. His mum, Lady Churchill, really was a Yank. She married well, of course."

But that wasn't the only American connection to Blenheim Palace, I learned. Consuelo, the 9th Duchess of Marlborough, and one of the mistresses of Blenheim Palace, was also an American – and a well known one at that. Her maiden name? Vanderbilt. Yes, *those* Vanderbilts.

Apparently, being a beautiful young woman from a wealthy American family in the late 19th century was sometimes just not enough. If you really wanted to make the neighbors green with envy, you and your parents headed off to Europe so that they could find you a husband with a title – just like in the Edith Wharton novel *The Buccaneers*.

"I hope you don't have similar designs," Kevin said mischievously. "I'm just a boring commoner."

"You mean you're not secretly Viscount Clue, with a vast estate and a huge fortune? It's all right to let the secret out now. I've always thought I'd make a nice countess."

"I'm afraid you'll have to keep daydreaming or find yourself a real viscount. There's not a drop of royal blood in this body."

Blenheim Palace was on the way to our third destination: Stratford-upon-Avon. After having spent the previous eight months in a class devoted entirely to Shakespeare, I was finally going to see where he was born, went to school, and married. In fact, this was the highlight of any English major's must-see list. I could barely contain my excitement as Kevin pulled into the driveway of The Hollies, the B+B that I had booked us into. Then I remembered that I had to tell Kevin something important about our accommodations.

"Oh, uh, before we go inside, I need to tell you that we're Mr. and Mrs. Clue for this part of our trip." I tried to sound as casual as I could.

"I beg your pardon?" he replied. He watched in amusement as I took off the sapphire birthstone ring that I wore on the wedding finger of my left hand and put it in my lap. Then he started to laugh as I removed my MHC ring from my right hand, put it on my left wedding finger, and spun it around so that only the thick gold band showed. I put my birthstone ring back on my left hand so that it now looked like I was wearing a small engagement ring and wedding band.

"I can't wait to hear why you're doing this," Kevin said.

"Well, when I made the room booking, I gave the lady your last name because it's shorter and easier to spell than mine is. At the end of the phone call she said, 'We're so looking forward to welcoming you, Mrs. Clue.' She sounded so cute and proper that I didn't have the heart to correct her and tell her the truth."

"You mean you didn't want her to know we're living in sin for two weeks, as your mum would say. Do you really think our host cares about that?"

"I don't know. My *Let's Go* said that the B+B is run by two spinster sisters. I didn't want to take chances in case they frowned on an unmarried couple traveling together. Are you mad at me?"

"Of course not. I think you spend way too much time worrying about things, though. I'll bet they don't even take notice." We got our bags out of the car and walked up to the front door. Before we could even ring the bell, the door opened and we were greeted by a small, neatly dressed woman with snow-white hair that was gathered into a tidy bun at the top of her head.

"Welcome to the Hollies! You must be Mr. and Mrs. Clue," she said happily. "And so young – you must be newlyweds! Let me show you to your room." I didn't dare look at Kevin as we followed our host up the front stairs because I was afraid I'd start laughing.

In Stratford, we hit most of the major sights on the Shakespeare circuit: The Bard's birthplace, Anne Hathaway's cottage, and New Place, where Shakespeare retired. And of course, I dragged Kevin with me on the pilgrimage to Holy Trinity Church, where Shakespeare was baptized and is buried. To my surprise, his gravesite was quite modest and unassuming, considering his fame at the time of his death. But it was worth the visit just to read his epitaph:

Good friend for Jesus sake forebeare,/To digg the dust encloased heare./Blese [blest] be ye man yt [that] spares thes stones,/And curst be he yt [that] moves my bones.

"What exactly does that mean?" Kevin asked.

"It means that he didn't want to be dug up and moved to the charnel house."

"And what is a charnel house, please?"

"It's a building where your bones were moved after you'd been buried in a churchyard or a church and your body had decomposed. That way, the space could be re-used for another burial."

"Oh, thanks. I wish I hadn't asked."

"See what you've missed by being an Accounting and Maths major?"

I was so impressed with Shakespeare's epitaph that I bought a life-size poster of it made from a rubbing of the original.

"That's a bit ghoulish, don't you think?" Kevin questioned.

"Are you kidding? I think it's great. It's like he's daring people to mess with him after he's gone. I love it! It'll look great in my dorm room back at Mount Holyoke this fall."

Now I'd done it – I'd mentioned going home, and Kevin and I had made a promise that we weren't going to talk about my return to the States until it was time to head to the airport.

"Sorry – I forgot. I was just thinking about what I'd do with the poster."

"Don't worry about it. You know, we should probably head over to the RSC to pick up our tickets for tonight's play."

"RSC" is short for the Royal Shakespeare Company, which is known for its extremely imaginative (some purists might call them irreverent) interpretations of Shakespeare's plays. For example, one production of "Romeo and Juliet" featured the feuding Montague and Capulet families zipping about the stage on Vespa scooters. I personally think Shakespeare would've gotten a huge kick out of the RSC's inventiveness.

Some of England's most distinguished actors – including Dame Judi Dench, Jeremy Irons, Alan Rickman, Kenneth Branagh, Dame Helen Mirren, Vanessa Redgrave, and Sir Ben Kingsley – are RSC alums. Unfortunately, nobody we saw in that night's production went on to become a famous film star. But we still enjoyed a spellbinding performance.

After we got out of the theatre, we walked all the way around the huge basin in Stratford's center where the Stratford Canal and River Avon meet. Stratford is a major hub in England's vast network of canals. Once used as watery highways for industrial barges, these canals now serve pleasure craft called narrowboats.

<table>
<tr><td>Say what?
Brit/Yank Translator</td><td>**Narrowboats:** houseboats</td></tr>
</table>

Moored in the basin were all kinds of narrowboats; some of them were on the shorter side and others were nearly as long as a bus. Many had pots filled with beautiful flowers or tomato plants along their flat roofs. Party lanterns were strung along their sides or at their front entrances. And all of them were brightly painted with their own color schemes.

A typical narrowboat.

"I just love these boats," I said to Kevin, as we walked past one particularly festive-looking narrowboat. I bent down to peer in the window through an open lace curtain. "They're like floating RVs. Oh look - this one has a phone number and a company name painted on the outside. Does that mean you can rent them?"

"Yes, that one there is a holiday let."

"Wouldn't that be fun to go on a canal vacation? We should do that someday."

"I did it once as a scout," Kevin said with a smile. "It's not all relaxation – you have to work the canal locks yourself and pilot the boat through the gates. It's quite hard work, but brilliant fun. Especially if the weather is fine. Mind you, that boat you're looking at now is rather more posh than the one our scout troop hired."

"Oh?"

"We were packed in like sardines and cooked all of our meals in the galley."

"Galley?" I asked.

"Boat talk for 'kitchen.' Anyway, the renters of this narrowboat in front of us are probably not using their galley very much, I reckon. I'll bet they're enjoying a gourmet dinner in one of Stratford's restaurants right now." He started to laugh. "We came back from our canal holiday absolutely filthy – but what do you expect from a load of 10-year-old boys and dads who didn't have mums on board telling them to bathe?!"

The center of Stratford was beautiful. On one side of the basin was the RSC theater. On the opposite side were the Bancroft Gardens, with beautiful walking paths, mature trees, and flower gardens. In the gardens was the Gower Memorial, which is actually a grouping of one large statue (Shakespeare) surrounded by four smaller statues of his more well-known characters: Prince Hal, Hamlet, Falstaff, and Lady Macbeth. I walked around the Memorial checking out all of the statues. Suddenly, from behind me, I heard Kevin laughing loudly.

"Diane – over here. Look!" More laughing.

I turned around to see him standing at the Hamlet statue, which depicts the Prince of Denmark staring contemplatively at the skull from the famous "Alas, poor Yorick" scene of the play. The statue Hamlet, who is sitting down, leans his head against one hand while he holds the skull in the other. It's a dramatic moment in the play. But what I was looking at right now would, I imagine, have poor Shakespeare spinning in his modest grave. There stood Kevin – with his finger strategically placed up the seated Hamlet's nose.

"Oh my God, Kevin!" I shouted. "Stop picking Hamlet's nose! I can't believe you're doing that. It's sacrilege. You – you – *Philistine!*"

Kevin didn't remove his finger. Instead, he tried to look extremely serious (inasmuch as one can look serious with one's finger up Hamlet's nose), cleared his throat, and solemnly announced, "To be or not to be...."

"That's not even the right scene from the play!"

"Get thee to a nunnery."

"Wrong scene again! Cut it out! He's your own countryman, for God's sake."

"Actually, my little English major, Hamlet was a Dane. Tsk, tsk. You of all people should know that."

"I wasn't talking about Hamlet and you know it! I meant Shakespeare. Now get your finger out of Hamlet's nose." A few tourists walked by, took one look at the scene that was unfolding, and started to smile.

"Don't I at least get points for quoting some lines from the play?" Kevin was clearly enjoying this. He smirked and left his finger exactly where it was.

"O.K., you get a couple of points. Now quit it."

"Not until you take a photo. Go on, you know you want to."

"Fine! I'll take the stupid photo. There, now will you please act normal?" But he had worn me down. I started to laugh. "Can't I take you anywhere?" I asked as we left Bancroft Gardens and started to walk back to The Hollies.

"Of course you can. But years from now, when you look at that photo, you'll remember how fun and spontaneous I was."

"If you say so."

Kevin was right, of course. When I got the film developed after I'd arrived home in the States, the infamous Hamlet picture ended up being the shot that made me laugh out loud.

Alas, poor Hamlet.

✧ Chapter Twenty-Six ✧

On our way from Stratford-upon-Avon back to Petersfield, Kevin surprised me with a stop at Warwick Castle, whose history stretches back nearly 1,100 years. He said it was a fairytale English castle that he was sure I would fall in love with. It was, and I did. We spent the better part of the day there. The entire place is like something out of a child's storybook, and I half-expected to see knights in suits of armor appear along the ramparts and in the keep at any moment.

Peacocks and peahens wandered around the lawns and perched in the trees; their eerie, almost human cries echoed all over the property, and they were completely unfazed by all the people around them. In fact, they strolled right up to us. The peacocks spread out their tails as if to say, "Hey, check me out." They even posed for pictures.

In addition to exploring the castle and its gorgeous grounds, we saw a falconry demonstration and another one that featured archery. We also saw a modern-day replica of a trebuchet, a fearsome medieval battle weapon, in action. And we had a relaxing picnic lunch along the bank of the River Avon that bends near the castle's east side.

Late in the afternoon, as we were leaving, we experienced one final thing that I could only describe as surreal: a dance performed by fully grown men in sky-blue stockings who wore matching hats piled with fresh flowers. From the backs of their hats cascaded long ribbons that were the same shade as the men's tights.

The performers danced in formations and waved sticks in their hands — the sticks were wrapped in ribbons whose colors matched the flowers in the men's hats. Bright sashes criss-crossed the men's white shirts and contrasted with their black breeches. Multicolored garlands around the men's necks completed the spectacle. Three musicians on an accordion, drum, and fiddle played the tune that the men were dancing to. I was astonished. A Monty Python sketch had come to life right before my eyes.

Morris Dancers at Warwick Castle.

"What on earth are we watching right now?" I asked Kevin.

"Morris Dancers. It's an old type of English folk dance. There are Morris Men groups all over England."

The performance ended, everyone broke into applause, and the dancers began circulating through the crowd of spectators. One of the men walked straight up to me. "Hello, luv," he said. "And did you enjoy the performance?"

"I've never seen anything like it," I replied with complete honesty.

"Ah, an American visitor. There are some Morris Men groups in the States, you know. You'll have to see if you can find one near you when you return. Here you are, my darling." He pulled a bright yellow flower out of his hat and handed it to me with a flourish.

I turned bright-red, to Kevin's great amusement.

Two days later we were in Paris, on the final leg of our Grand Tour. We had crossed the English Channel on a hovercraft, which was faster and smoother than the traditional ferries. I'd never been on one before, and it was like riding on a giant air-hockey puck (not that I've ever done that). From Calais, where we landed, we took a coach into Paris.

Our hotel – the Hotel des Arts – was an adorable two-star place on a tiny, quiet side street in the Ninth Arrondissement. It was only a short walk from the Rue Montmartre stop on the Paris Metro. But the best part was the parrot in the hotel's lobby. It was something of a local celebrity. When we first arrived to check in, we walked by its cage, an ornate metal creation suspended from a tall floor stand. As I passed, the parrot let loose with a loud wolf-whistle. I nearly jumped out of my skin.

But the parrot had other talents, too. As it sat and watched the world go by from the open lobby door that looked out into the street, it cheerily whistled the first bar of "La Marseillaise," the French national anthem. Kevin, however, decided the bird needed to expand its repertoire. When we walked by the cage the next morning, Kevin stopped and loudly whistled the first bar of "God Save the Queen," the U.K.'s national anthem.

"You're going to get us kicked out," I said jokingly. "Try whistling 'The Star-Spangled Banner' too. It won't look so obvious that way."

"It has to learn 'God Save the Queen' first," Kevin answered. He continued to whistle the beginning of the song to the parrot, who looked unimpressed and gave him a blank stare.

"I don't think it likes you."

At this, the landlady of the hotel, who had been watching us with interest from the front desk, came out from behind her post and joined us at the cage.

"*C'est un perroquet intelligent, Madame,*" I commented.

"*Ah oui, c'est vrai, mademoiselle,*" she replied with a nod. "*Mais c'est un perroquet francais. Il ne comprend pas anglais.*" Her eyes twinkled.

"*Touché, Madame,*" I said with a grin.

"What are you two going on about?" asked Kevin, who was determined to convert the bird.

"I told her she has a very smart parrot, and she agreed. But she also said that it's a French parrot, so it doesn't understand English." The landlady and I tried to keep straight faces, but failed miserably.

"Oh, very funny indeed, ladies. I'll have this parrot singing for Queen and country by the time we leave."

This became the running joke during our stay at the hotel. Every time we passed the cage, Kevin would whistle "God Save the Queen" and the parrot would impertinently reply with "La Marseillaise." The landlady would cheer and clap for her pet, and we'd all have a good laugh.

I wish I could say that all the Parisians we encountered were just as friendly as the woman at our hotel. We had heard that the residents here could be notoriously rude to visitors, but I was still optimistic. At the time of our visit I could speak French pretty well, so I certainly wasn't the stereotypical Ugly American who ran around shouting English at everyone. I was excited to have several days to use my second language, and I loved France's history and culture almost as much as I did England's.

Unfortunately, some of the staff in the restaurants, shops, and museums we visited were rude or just plain indifferent. One waiter at an outdoor café corrected my French to my face. Another Frenchman went so far as to pretend not to understand my French when I politely asked him for directions. I suddenly remembered what one of Kevin's friends had said when we'd told him we were going to Paris for a few days. He'd remarked archly, "Paris would be perfect if it weren't for the Parisians." Ouch.

Interestingly, in July of 2007 – exactly 20 years after Kevin and I visited The City of Lights – the Paris tourist office spearheaded an initiative that was aimed at encouraging Parisians to be more polite and welcoming to tourists. We felt belatedly vindicated. Sort of.

Despite some Parisians' reputations for giving tourists the cold shoulder, Kevin and I had an incredible time in the city. The weather was perfect, with sunny skies, warm days, and beautiful nights. We lost track of how many outdoor cafes we went to, and got hooked on *pain au chocolat.* So it's just as well that we walked all over Paris. Sure, it was fun riding the Metro, but we didn't want to miss a thing by being stuck underground, especially with such gorgeous weather. Unless our destinations for the day were terribly far apart, we consulted our maps and hoofed it. We must've walked 7-8 miles every day, judging by our aching feet each night.

Since we weren't sure when we'd return to Paris, we tried to take in all the major sights, like Notre Dame, the Eiffel Tower (Kevin called it the "Awful" Tower), the Place de la Concorde, the Arc de Triomphe, and Sacre-Coeur. We also managed to visit the house of one of my favorite French authors, Victor Hugo, as well as the Rodin Museum, the Moulin Rouge, and the Champs-Elysees.

And then there was the Louvre. Ask anyone who's visited this former royal palace – the word "huge" doesn't even begin to describe its size. You could spend an entire two-week vacation in the Louvre and still not see everything. So before we'd left England for Paris, we'd carefully sat down and made a list of the works we most wanted to see. Then we'd looked at the map of the Louvre to see where everything was located. Thanks to that careful planning, we were able to find and see the Venus de Milo, the Victory of Samothrace, Michaelangelo's "Slaves" sculptures, and the Mona Lisa.

The thing that surprised me the most about the Mona Lisa was how small the painting was. When you see such a famous work in art books, you automatically assume it's a large canvas. Coming face-to-face with the Mona Lisa's almost life-size head made her more real to me. We instantly knew we were in the right section of the museum when we saw a crowd standing silently in front of the painting. It has that kind of effect on you.

Even with the full day that we spent inside the Louvre, we barely made a dent in the museum. Once we'd had our fill of artwork, we left the museum and had the most decadent picnic dinner on the lawns of the adjoining Tuileries Gardens. These sprawling grounds are Paris's oldest and biggest public park. The French certainly know how to do outdoor spaces on a grand scale; there were walking paths, clipped lawns, benches, flower plantings, statues, trees, hedges, and even an ornamental lake. Our escape to Paris was the perfect way to end my junior year abroad. And as often as it's been said before, the city was truly one of the most romantic places I'd ever visited. We reluctantly headed back to England.

Once we arrived in Petersfield, there was no avoiding the inevitable. In just two short days I'd be flying back to the States. What had been the most amazing year of my life was coming to a close. And at the airport, I'd have to say the most difficult goodbye of all. Just thinking about it started me crying.

On the morning of July 8th, Kevin and I loaded my suitcases into his car for the final time and left for Heathrow. I was already a basket case, having spent a sleepless, tearful night in my room. More than once over the past few weeks, I had considered doing what one of my fellow American exchange students had done. I could stay here in England and transfer to UKC, buying myself another year in Canterbury with Kevin and my friends.

But then what? I knew it was an unrealistic plan. Once I'd earned my degree in England, I'd still have to go back to the States – unless I tried to go for a Master's degree program at Cambridge or Oxford. Hell, I didn't even know if I wanted a Master's. The only subject about which I was passionate enough to devote two years of my life was Shakespeare. And let's be honest: did the world really need another Shakespearean scholar?

Besides, I already had my summer job lined up at home; I'd be starting next week. I'd also selected my classes for my senior year at Mount Holyoke. My dorm room and my Mount Holyoke friends would be waiting for me in Buckland Hall come September. And in less than twelve hours, I'd be reunited with my parents, sisters, and Kim at Logan Airport. There was no way around it.

"Don't go getting all quiet on me already," Kevin said, breaking the silence. "We only just got on the road."

"I'm sorry." I bit my tongue as hard as I could so I wouldn't start crying. "I'm just thinking about how much I want to stay. This sucks."

"I know." Kevin gripped the steering wheel hard. His knuckles were white.

"Are you serious about wanting to come to Boston during Christmas break, or are you just trying to make me feel better?"

"I've never been more serious about anything. The time will fly by – you'll see. Before you know it, Christmas will be here and we'll be together again. After that it'll be only a short time until spring break, and you can spend it with all of us in England."

I knew that Kevin was trying to look on the bright side, but all I could see were long stretches of months apart. What if he met someone on this Spanish vacation that he was going on later this summer? What if he started dating someone at UKC when he went back in October? What if he just got tired of having a long-distance girlfriend? My lip started to tremble and my eyes began to water.

"Now, you promised me you wouldn't start crying until we got to passport control. Don't you go back on your word, Diane," Kevin warned.

"Sorry. O.K., I promise."

"Good. Oh look – there are some sheep in that field over there. So how many photos of those stupid creatures did you take over the past ten months, anyway? Are all Americans obsessed with sheep, or is it just you?"

"Well, Kathy, Julie, Sharolyn, and I thought they were cute. Especially the lambs. I guess we *did* take tons of pictures of them."

It was true. I didn't grow up in a farming community, so it was pretty cool seeing sheep all over the place in England. There were as common in the fields over here as squirrels were back home. Despite that, every time my friends and I saw sheep, whether they were in the fields around the university or we spotted them from the windows of a train, we'd still excitedly yell, "Look! Sheeeeeep!" More often than not, we'd take a picture.

"You do know that they're just about the dumbest animals on earth, don't you?" Kevin said. He spoke from experience, having spent a week working with his friend Mark on a sheep farm in Wales when they were schoolboys. "They don't even have the sense to come in out of bad weather. Useless things, if you ask me, although they are nice with mint sauce."

"You're awful!"

"Made you laugh, though."

An hour later we arrived at Heathrow. My stomach was in knots. Kevin pulled up to the entrance of the parking garage and came to a sudden stop. His face went ashen. *Oh no*, I thought. *Don't you start. I'll completely lose it now.*

"You wouldn't happen to have any cash on you, by any chance?" he asked.

"No. I used it all at the pub last night, remember?"

"Then we have a bit of a problem. I seem to have left my wallet back in Petersfield." Kevin patted his front and back pants pockets just to make sure, then looked at me nervously.

"Oh my God. Please tell me you are joking."

"Quite serious, I'm afraid. Well, this certainly is a spot of bother, isn't it?"

"A spot of bother?! That's an understatement! If we don't have any money, then we can't park the car. And if we can't park the car, then you'll have to leave me at the curb!" I started to come unglued; I wasn't ready to say goodbye to Kevin yet. He was supposed to stay with me all the way to passport control until right before I boarded my plane. I started to sweat and I was pretty sure I was going to break out in hives at any moment.

"Okay, okay – keep your hair on."

"Don't tell me to keep my hair on! You're the one who forgot your wallet!"

"Yes, well, reminding me is not helping the situation right now. And neither is yelling. There's no one behind us queuing to get in. Quick, dump out your handbag – there must be some change at the bottom of it. I'll search the car."

I got out of the car, frantically emptied my bag onto the road, and inspected the contents. I spotted a 50p coin and a few 10p ones. "This is it," I said, handing it over to Kevin and cramming everything else back into my purse.

"Lovely, thanks – I found some change between the car seats and under one of the floor mats. Let's see how much we have now." He walked up to the sign at the garage entrance that displayed the hourly rates. "That's lucky – we can pay for an hour. That should be enough time for me to wait with you at check-in, walk you straight to passport control, and run back here. Crisis averted. See?" He grinned.

"It's really hard to be angry with you when you smile like that."

"I know."

One look at the Departures screen confirmed that my flight from London to Boston was leaving on time. Not that Kevin could've paid for a longer stay at the parking garage even if there'd been a delay. An hour was an hour. By the time I was done checking my suitcases, we needed to head immediately to passport control. There would be no time for a last cup of tea, although at this stage a pint of the strongest cider available (or maybe even a snake bite) would've been way more welcome.

Hand in hand, Kevin and I approached the sign that announced, "TICKETED PASSENGERS ONLY BEYOND THIS POINT" and stepped off to the side so we wouldn't be in other people's way. I put down my purse and carry-on and threw my arms around Kevin's neck. Then I buried my head in his shoulder and started to cry. "I don't want to say goodbye...I can't," I bawled. The words came out in loud, long hiccupping sobs. It was hard to catch my breath.

Kevin held me tight. "It's not goodbye, Diane. We're going to see each other in just a few months. We can write and phone each other until then."

"It w-won't be the sa-a-a-me," I wailed inconsolably.

"But it will be enough. Please don't cry. I can't stand to watch you leave like this." He waited until I came up for air, and then loosened my grip on his neck so he could take my hands and look me in the eyes. "Think of how much fun we'll have when I come out for Christmas break. Now please give me a kiss and get on that plane. I'll see you when I see you."

"I guess that's better than goodbye," I snuffled as I wiped my nose. "This has been the best year of my life."

"It's just the start. I promise."

"I love you, Kevin. Thank you. For everything."

"I love you, too. Now off you go."

I bent down to pick up my purse and carry-on, walked tearfully through passport control, and began the long journey home.

✧ Epilogue ✧

I don't know if there's any official name for what I experienced when I came back to the States, but I unofficially dubbed it "reverse culture shock." It hit me hard, and I was completely unprepared for it. I'd so successfully immersed myself into my life in England that I had a terrible time getting "re-Americanized"– although it was wonderful to enjoy real, full-blast showers and toasted meatball grinders again.

All kidding aside, my first semester back at Mount Holyoke was a tough one. My closest friends hadn't studied abroad, so they didn't get what I was going through. I missed Kevin and all of the English friends I'd left behind in Canterbury. I cried a lot, threw myself into my studies, and spent a lot of time alone in my dorm room.

What did make that awful first semester more bearable was knowing that Kathy, Julie, Sharolyn, and Bob were going through the exact same thing. We spent a lot of time writing and calling each other in the months that followed our "re-entry," as we referred to it.

By the time Christmas of my senior year at Mount Holyoke had arrived, I'd decided that I wasn't done with England. Not by a long shot. Kevin and the rest of the C Block crew were now second-years; that meant they would be graduating in Canterbury Cathedral the following year. I wanted to do more than just fly out and watch their graduation as a guest. I wanted to be there for their third year, just as I'd done with their first year. I got an idea.

I tracked down Robin – the Mount Holyoke graduate who'd been doing a work abroad program in London during my year at

UKC – and asked her to tell me everything she could about the program. Did you have to work and live in London, or could you go anywhere in the U.K.? How long could you stay? When I heard her answers, I quickly made up my mind. I'd spend the 1988-89 school year back in Canterbury, except this time around I'd live there as a working person and not as a student. Great! Now all I had to do was find a job and a place to live.

But I'm getting ahead of myself. That's a subject for another book....

✧ Author's Notes ✧

More than 25 years have passed since I first arrived at UKC. A lot has changed since then. For example, the university did away with the old Michaelmas, Lent, and Trinity term names. A three-term academic calendar still exists, though with the more secular names of Autumn, Spring, and Summer.

The campus itself has grown tremendously, with new student housing options and academic buildings. Areas that were playing fields and open space in my student days are now the sites of a new college (Woolf) and new student apartments (Darwin Houses). Parkwood Court has been expanded, too.

Only one "traditional" dining hall – the one in Rutherford College – remains now. The halls at the other three original colleges were converted into academic space or were remodeled into snack bars, restaurants, and other dining choices that better suit modern students' lifestyles.

Students at UKC – and there are thousands more of them today than there were in the 1980s – can take advantage of incredible technological resources and learning tools that were only in their infancy when I was an undergraduate.

But some things haven't changed at all. Today's students can still enjoy a pint at The Gate or The Dog and Bear (although the latter now goes by the name of "The Dog @ Rough Common"). They can go out to dinner at some of the same restaurants where my friends and I ate, including The Old Weavers House and Marlowe's. And they are still awed and inspired by Canterbury's majestic cathedral.

Spending my junior year abroad was a great adventure at the time, but it wasn't until I got back to the States that I understood what that year really did for me. The U.S. is such a huge place that it's easy for a young person to think it's the center of the universe. I was as guilty of that as any other American student.

But studying abroad changes you. Among other things, you realize you don't need nearly as much "stuff" as you thought you did. You see yourself through someone else's world view. You become way more curious and a lot less critical. And you experience the thrill of calling another country "home."

I can't think of a better gift to give yourself.

✧ Acknowledgments ✧

My dear friend Colin Harris — the first English friend I made during my junior year abroad — never lived to see this book become a reality. Sadly, he passed away in 1998. In the years that followed UKC, Colin and I remained close. We visited each other often. Whenever we got together, he would relentlessly grill me on when I was going to get around to writing "the UKC book," as he called it. "Someday," I'd promise. I wish I hadn't taken so long to keep that promise.

I'm grateful to so many other people who helped make *A Broad Abroad* a reality.

To Linda Dini Jenkins, my book midwife and editor extraordinaire, "thanks" falls woefully short of the mark. Over the years she has been a wonderful boss, a thoughtful friend, a wise mentor, a calm voice of reason, and an inspiring example of what "successful" really means. Linda's terrific suggestion to add the "Say What?" and "Know Before You Go" sections completely transformed this book.

The enormously talented Holly Mason, of Mason Design, turned a Word document, a stack of photos, and a pile of memorabilia into the gorgeous book you're holding in your hands.

Although I've never met him personally, Chris Baty, the founder of National Novel Writing Month (NaNoWriMo) provided the virtual kick in the pants that I needed to finally get my book out of my head and into my computer's hard drive. His hilarious book *No Plot? No Problem! A Low-Stress, High-Velocity Guide to Writing a Novel in 30 Days* was a huge source of practical advice.

My mom and dad have always encouraged me to dream big. When I decided at the age of 10 that I wanted to become the first altar girl at St. Cecilia's Catholic Church, they replied, "Go for it." When I told them I had my sights set on getting into an Ivy League college, they said, "You can do it." And when I decided to quit my secure, full-time job to become a freelance writer, they said, "Congratulations! You'll be great at it." Thank you, Mom and Dad, for never once telling me to play it safe.

Finally, I'd like to thank my husband Kevin – my best souvenir from my junior year abroad – and our son Domenic. They cheered me on as I participated in NaNoWriMo 2009. They left me alone in my office so that I could write in peace. They did the grocery shopping and didn't complain when the dirty laundry piled up. And they encouraged me to keep writing, even on the days when I didn't think I had 1,667 words in me.

All of these people made the seemingly impossible, well – possible.

I am blessed indeed.

Upton, MA
September 2010

www.abroadabroadjya.com